WHEN WORK BECOMES WAR

Healing from Workplace Bullying and Betrayal

VERONICA RUFF

Integrity Press Australia

Contents

Part II

Systems, Patterns, and Reform

Part VIII

The Systemic Mirror

Part IX

Generational Impact

Part III

Psychological Insight and Recovery

Part IV

Scenes from the Reckoning

Part V

Appendices

Disclaimer

This book is based on the author's lived experience. Names, institutions, and identifying details have been changed to protect privacy. The workplace environments described are authentic to the author's experience.

Psychological profiles and behavioural patterns referenced throughout reflect dynamics commonly observed in toxic workplaces. They are not clinical diagnoses, but behavioural descriptions drawn from lived reality.

This work is not intended to substitute for professional legal, medical, or psychological advice. Readers are encouraged to seek qualified support where needed.

DEDICATION

For everyone who
was silenced—
and for everyone who refused
to stay that way.
 For those who were called too
sensitive, too intense, too much—
and still chose clarity over comfort.
 For the ones rebuilding in quiet
rooms, writing truth in the margins
of their own lives.
 This book is for you.
 You were never the problem.
 You were the pattern-breaker.

Veronica Ruff

Note on the Illustrations

These illustrations are not depictions
of events but reflections of truth.
They appear as moments of stillness
— breaths between the heavier pages —
invitations to pause, to feel, to remember
that clarity can exist beside pain.
Each image carries the quiet pulse of reclamation: the knowing that
art can hold what words cannot.
They do not explain.
They simply witness.
(All artwork © Veronica Ruff)

Foreword

By a trauma-informed psychologist (name withheld for privacy)
In my years of clinical practice and organisational consulting, I've witnessed the silent epidemic of workplace trauma — where cruelty is cloaked in professionalism, and emotional abuse is reframed as *feedback*. Few have named it with the clarity, courage, and emotional precision that Veronica does in these pages.

This isn't just a book.

It is a reckoning.

Veronica's work accomplishes what most HR manuals, leadership seminars, and institutional policies fail to do: it tells the truth. It names the choreography of harm — gaslighting, triangulation, sabotage — and honours the survivor's nervous system, voice, and legacy. It is both testimony and toolkit, both mirror and medicine.

What makes this work extraordinary is not only its emotional resonance but its editorial integrity. Every case study is framed with care. Every glossary term is defined with nuance. Every cartoon, reflection, and chapter builds toward a singular truth: that recovery is not about returning to who you were, but about becoming who you were always meant to be.

This is a resource for survivors, advocates, clinicians, and anyone who has ever felt erased by a system that rewards silence. It is fierce, poetic, and unflinching. It does not ask for permission to speak — it speaks because it must.

To read this book is to walk beside a truth-teller; to witness the cost of cruelty and the power of reclamation; to remember that clarity is not conflict, and boundaries are not betrayal.

Veronica has not simply written a book. She has built a sanctuary.

Let this be a place of recognition, restoration, and return.

Prologue

LEGACY STATEMENT

This book is a testament to the resilience of those who have endured what others refuse to name. It is not merely food for thought — it is a call to awareness, a mirror held up to the systems we navigate, and a reminder that truth, once spoken, cannot be silenced.

I did not choose this path — I was pushed onto it by cruelty, sabotage, and silence. I walked into rooms where no one knew me, yet the lies had already arrived. I was shunned before I could speak, judged before I could show, and punished for the light I carried.

I grieve the career I could have had, the self I used to be — the one who was carefree, wanted, and whole. I mourn the loss of dignity, the panic attacks, the lowered self-esteem, the fear of being crucified again in public spaces. I will never be the same person I used to be. The effects are lasting and life-changing, but I have learned to adapt to a new way of being.

One of the cruellest feelings in life is not to be wanted — and I have been made to feel that way many times. To the workplaces that ignored me, and to those responsible for doing this not only to me but to many others: the weight of truth will find its way.

To the survivors — yes, to all of us — we have travelled the paths of isolation, of injustice, of being unseen. But we have also travelled the paths of truth, of courage, of reclaiming our voices. We are not who we were, yet we are still here. We are still standing.

This book is not only a record of what happened — it is a reckoning. It names what others deny. It speaks what others silence. It holds the mirror up to systems that failed the soul.

To those who read this and feel seen: you are not alone.

To those who caused this and feel exposed: the truth is now yours to carry.

I leave this work not as a victim, but as a witness. Not as someone erased, but as someone who endured. Not as someone broken, but as someone who chose to speak.

This is my legacy — truth, named and unflinching.

May it echo in every room where silence once reigned.

Tools, Language, and Restoration

PART V

Glossary of Terms

This glossary defines key terms used throughout this book to support clarity, emotional resonance, and shared understanding.

Boundary-Setting: The act of defining and asserting personal limits to protect emotional, physical, and psychological wellbeing.

Bullying: Repeated, harmful behaviour — verbal, emotional, or psychological — intended to intimidate, undermine, or isolate an individual.

Clarity: The state of seeing, naming, and understanding patterns, behaviours, and truths without distortion.

Conditional Affection: Offering love, support, or approval only when someone complies with expectations or demands.

Containment: A system's response to truth-telling that seeks to suppress, deflect, or neutralise the speaker rather than address the harm.

Emotional Abuse: Non-physical behaviour that harms emotional wellbeing, including invalidation, control, criticism, and manipulation.

Emotional Regulation: The ability to manage and respond to emotional experiences in a healthy, grounded way.

Erasure: The act of ignoring, invalidating, or removing someone's contributions, presence, or truth.

Fawning: A trauma response in which an individual seeks to appease or please others to avoid conflict, disapproval, or harm — often at the expense of their own needs, boundaries, or identity.

'Feedback' (in toxic contexts): A term often used to disguise sabotage, criticism, or manipulation under the guise of professional development.

Gaslighting: A form of psychological manipulation in which someone denies your reality, rewrites events, or makes you question your memory and instincts.

Human Resources (HR): A department intended to support employee wellbeing and workplace fairness but which, in toxic cultures, may serve to protect management and suppress complaints.

Legacy: The lasting impact of one's truth, story, and healing — often shaped through creative expression, advocacy, and testimony.

Microaggressions: Subtle, often unintentional behaviours or comments that convey bias, exclusion, or disrespect.

Narcissist: A person who craves admiration and control, often charming at first but dismissive or cruel when their ego is threatened.

Performative Loyalty: Superficial allegiance to a person or system, used to gain favour rather than reflect genuine integrity.

Psychological Safety: A workplace condition in which individuals feel safe to express themselves without fear of punishment, ridicule, or retaliation.

Reclamation: The process of reclaiming one's voice, truth, and dignity after being silenced or erased.

Recovery: The emotional, psychological, and physical process of healing after trauma, betrayal, or systemic harm.

Sabotage: Deliberate actions intended to undermine, obstruct, or harm another's work, reputation, or wellbeing.

Self-Compassion: Treating oneself with kindness, patience, and understanding — especially after harm or betrayal.

Silent Treatment: Withholding communication as a form of punishment or control.

Sociopath: An individual who lacks empathy and uses relationships strategically for manipulation and personal gain.

Sovereignty: The act of reclaiming personal power, truth, and autonomy after being silenced or manipulated.

Toxic Workplace: An environment where dysfunction, manipulation, and emotional harm are normalised — often protected by systems that reward silence and punish truth.

Triangulation: A tactic used to control or manipulate by involving a third party to create confusion, division, or emotional instability.

Workplace Psychopath: A person who mimics empathy to gain trust, then exploits others with calculated cruelty — often thriving in systems that reward appearance over substance.

If You're Struggling...

If you are struggling, please know this: what happened to you was **not your fault**.

The psychological and physical wounds of workplace bullying are real, and they deserve the same care as any other trauma. The body remembers what the workplace denies — the tension, the exhaustion, the nights spent replaying conversations that stripped you of dignity.

You don't have to carry this on your own. Support is not weakness; it is a declaration of worth. Seek help from trauma-informed professionals, counsellors, or medical practitioners who understand workplace abuse as a form of psychological injury. If possible, document what has happened — even if you never use it. Writing your truth anchors it in reality.

When the noise of injustice grows too loud, find stillness where you can. Breathe. Rest. Nourish your nervous system with small acts of self-kindness: water, sunlight, movement, silence.

If you are in crisis or feel unsafe, reach out now — to a trusted friend, a helpline, or an emergency service. You do not have to be brave in isolation.

You're not overreacting and you're not imagining it.

Healing is not linear. It is slow, messy, and cyclical — but it is possible. The mere fact that you are reading this, seeking understanding, means the reclamation has already begun.

You are not alone. Workplace bullying can leave deep wounds — emotional, psychological, and physical — but healing is possible.

Whether you confide in a trusted friend, a trauma-informed counsellor, or a professional support service, reaching out is an act of courage and self-respect. You deserve safety, dignity, and care.

Support is not weakness; it is proof that you still believe in your own worth.

Support Services in Australia

Services:

Lifeline
Contact Information: 13 11 14
Focus: 24/7 crisis support and suicide prevention

Beyond Blue
Contact Information: 1300 22 4636
Focus: Mental health support and resources

1800RESPECT
Contact Information: 1800 737 732
Focus: Confidential counselling for abuse and bullying

Fair Work Ombudsman
Contact Information: 13 13 94
Focus: Workplace rights and bullying support

Safe Work Australia
Contact Information: safeworkaustralia.gov.au
Focus: Workplace health and safety guidance

Reaching out is not weakness — it is a powerful step toward reclaiming your wellbeing and your right to exist without fear. Each time you ask for help, you interrupt the silence that protects the system and begin to rebuild the one thing bullying tries to steal: **your sense of self**.

Types of Mental Abuse

Abuse is not always loud or visible. It often hides in words, silences, and patterns of control. Below are twelve common forms of mental and emotional abuse — each harmful, each deserving to be named.

Type	Description
Name-Calling	Using derogatory names or insults to demean and belittle.
Gaslighting	Influencing someone into questioning their own reality.
Character Assassination	Spreading false or malicious rumours about someone.
Isolation	Restricting someone's ability to socialise or communicate.
Threatening	Using intimidation or fear to control or manipulate.
Emotional Blackmail	Guilt-tripping or using someone's emotions against them.
Humiliation	Publicly or privately shaming or degrading someone.
Silent Treatment	Ignoring or giving someone the 'cold shoulder' as punishment.
Verbal Abuse	Yelling, screaming, or using aggressive language.
Invalidation	Dismissing or minimising someone's feelings or experiences.
Manipulation	Exploiting someone's vulnerabilities for personal gain.
Constant Criticism	Habitually pointing out flaws or mistakes.

Psychological Effects of Workplace Bullying

Workplace bullying leaves deep and lasting psychological scars. The following effects are commonly reported by those who have endured prolonged abuse in professional settings:

• **Anxiety and panic attacks:** Racing thoughts, heart palpitations, hypervigilance, and a constant sense of dread.
• **Depression and low self-esteem:** The gradual erosion of self-worth, accompanied by feelings of hopelessness and helplessness.
• **Post-Traumatic Stress responses:** Flashbacks, avoidance, hyperarousal, and emotional numbing.
• **Sleep disturbances:** Insomnia, nightmares, and disrupted or restless sleep.
• **Cognitive strain:** Difficulty concentrating, impaired decision-making, and mental fatigue.
• **Fawning and over-apologising:** A trauma-based urge to appease aggressors or minimise conflict, often at the cost of one's own truth or boundaries.
• **Paralysis and self-doubt:** An inability to make decisions or take action for fear of being targeted, blamed, or further humiliated.
• **Fear-based compliance:** Wanting to defend oneself yet feeling

trapped by the power dynamics that punish dissent and reward silence.

• **Social withdrawal:** Isolation from colleagues, friends, and family — often a protective response to betrayal and loss of trust.

• **Suicidal ideation:** In severe cases, thoughts of self-harm or despair when support systems are inadequate.

These are not merely emotional reactions; they are **traumatic imprints of chronic humiliation, exclusion, and fear**. Healing requires validation, rest, and environments where safety replaces surveillance — where boundaries, not appeasement, become the new language of belonging.

Physical Effects of Workplace Bullying

The psychological toll of bullying often manifests in the body. These physical symptoms may persist long after the bullying has stopped:

• **Muscle tension and headaches:** The body carries what the voice cannot yet speak.
• **Fatigue and exhaustion:** Constant emotional strain depletes the body's reserves.
• **Digestive issues:** Nausea, bloating, and irritable bowel symptoms linked to prolonged stress.
• **Appetite changes:** Overeating or loss of appetite as the nervous system swings between hyperarousal and shutdown.
• **Weakened immunity:** Increased susceptibility to colds, infections, and chronic illness.
• **Sleep disturbances:** Insomnia, restless sleep, or nightmares that mirror the mind's unrest.
• **Somatic memory:** Persistent pain or medical symptoms with no clear physical cause — the body remembering what the mind has tried to survive.

These effects ripple outward — undermining workplace culture, eroding productivity, and impacting home life and long-term health.

The damage does not end when the bullying stops; recovery begins only when truth is named and safety is restored — when the body, finally believed, is allowed to rest.

Reflection: The Body Remembers What the Mind Endured

The aftermath of workplace bullying is not simply emotional or physical — it is both, intertwined.

The mind learns to anticipate harm; the body learns to brace for it. Over time, this becomes muscle memory, cellular memory — a way of surviving what could not be spoken.

Healing, then, is not just about understanding what happened, but allowing the body to unlearn its fear.

Recovery begins when the nervous system feels safe enough to stop defending itself — when the story is named, the silence breaks, and the body is no longer asked to hold it alone.

Truths from the Trenches

The following reflections are drawn from lived experience and recurring patterns observed in toxic workplaces. They are not accusations, but insights — hard-won lessons from within systems that mistake cruelty for culture.

• **The quickest way to make good employees leave** is for managers to tolerate the behaviour of toxic staff with poor work ethics.
• **Toxic cultures reward loyalty to dysfunction over integrity.** Speaking up is punished; silence is rewarded.
• **In toxic workplaces, the most manipulative people often rise to power** — not because they are competent or ethical, but because they know how to play the game.
• **When leadership lacks emotional intelligence,** the workplace becomes a breeding ground for fear, resentment, and burnout.
• **Cruelty becomes normalised** when it is disguised as *"just business"* or *"tough love."*
• **The longer you stay in a toxic culture,** the more it erodes your self-worth and distorts your sense of reality.

• **Human Resources in toxic organisations** often functions as a shield for management rather than an advocate for employees.

• **The most dangerous thing about a toxic culture** is how it convinces good people that *they* are the problem.

• **Performative loyalty is rewarded over genuine contribution.** Those who flatter leadership are promoted, while truth-tellers are sidelined.

• **In dysfunctional systems, emotional abuse is reframed as "feedback,"** and psychological safety is dismissed as weakness.

• **Toxic workplaces rarely implode in one dramatic event.** They erode slowly — through daily microaggressions, silence, and systemic neglect.

• **When accountability is absent, cruelty becomes routine.** People stop asking *"Is this right?"* and start asking *"Will I get away with it?"*

• **The most insidious cultures are those that preach the values they betray** — diversity, integrity, care — while protecting abusers behind closed doors.

These are not opinions. They are observations born of endurance — truths carried by those who stayed long enough to see the cost of silence and the price of clarity.

Profiles of Predation

The following behavioural profiles reflect patterns commonly observed in toxic workplaces. They are not clinical diagnoses, but descriptive portraits drawn from lived experience and repeated observation.

• **Narcissists** crave admiration and control. They charm, flatter, and manipulate — then discard you the moment you no longer serve their ego.
• **Sociopaths** lack empathy and view relationships as strategic tools for manipulation. They calculate outcomes, conceal intent, and often operate behind the scenes.
• **Workplace psychopaths** are the most dangerous of all. They mimic empathy to gain trust, then weaponise it to exploit. Ruthless and deliberate, they advance through charm while concealing cruelty.

These individuals often target **high performers** — those who are competent, authentic, and unwilling to play games. Strength threatens them; integrity exposes them.

Tactics of Control

- **Gaslighting:** Twisting facts, denying reality, and making you question your memory, perception, and sanity.
- **Isolation:** Turning colleagues against you through gossip, lies, and subtle sabotage until you are alone and doubting yourself.
- **Chaos creation:** Thriving in environments where accountability is weak and appearances matter more than substance.
- **Domination over collaboration:** Viewing the workplace as a battlefield to be won, not a community to be nurtured.

Healing from their abuse begins with **distance, clarity, and the reclamation of your own worth.**

Advanced Manipulation Patterns

- **Triangulation:** Narcissists pit people against each other to maintain control and deflect attention from their own behaviour.
- **Mirrored empathy:** Sociopaths study your values and vulnerabilities, then mirror them back to you as a disguise — using your empathy to disarm and manipulate.
- **Charismatic cruelty:** Workplace psychopaths present as charming and competent, their malice masked by charisma. This makes them difficult to detect — and even harder for others to believe.
- **Exploitation of ambiguity:** They thrive in roles with vague responsibilities, minimal oversight, and maximum visibility — rewriting narratives unchecked.
- **Plausible deniability:** They say just enough to wound but never enough to be held accountable.
- **Psychological destabilisation:** Their goal is confusion, isolation, and self-doubt. When you question your instincts, they win.

Recovery from their abuse begins with **naming the pattern**, **reclaiming your voice**, and **refusing to internalise their**

projections. The truth is simple: you were not too sensitive, too ambitious, or too outspoken — you were simply inconvenient to their illusion of power.

Signs of a Bad Manager

The following behaviours are drawn from lived experience and repeated observation. They reveal the patterns commonly found in ineffective — and often harmful — managers. These traits not only corrode workplace morale, but also perpetuate cultures of fear, confusion, and emotional exhaustion.

• **Micromanagement:** Constant hovering, second-guessing, and controlling every task. What begins as "attention to detail" becomes a signal of mistrust and insecurity.
• **Favouritism:** Rewarding loyalty over competence. This creates division, fuels resentment, and silences dissenting voices.
• **Poor communication:** Withholding information, giving vague instructions, or failing to listen. Clarity is replaced by confusion; uncertainty becomes control.
• **Avoidance of accountability:** Blaming others for mistakes, deflecting responsibility, and refusing to apologise. These managers rewrite history to protect ego over integrity.
• **Inconsistency:** Changing expectations without warning or enforcing rules selectively. Employees are left walking on eggshells, unsure what version of leadership will appear each day.

• **Emotional volatility:** Mood swings, public outbursts, or passive-aggressive remarks that destabilise the team. Emotional safety evaporates under unpredictable leadership.

• **Sabotage of growth:** Blocking promotions, withholding opportunities, or subtly undermining confidence. These managers fear talent and punish ambition.

• **Dismissiveness:** Ignoring feedback, invalidating concerns, or belittling contributions. Dismissiveness is not efficiency — it is contempt disguised as authority.

• **Lack of empathy:** Failing to support staff during personal or professional challenges. Humanity becomes optional; performance is all that matters.

• **Gaslighting:** Denying events, twisting facts, or making employees doubt their own perceptions. In such environments, truth itself becomes negotiable.

These behaviours erode trust, morale, and psychological safety. They turn workplaces into arenas of survival rather than collaboration.

Naming these patterns is not an act of rebellion — it is an act of reclamation. Once named, they lose their power to define you.

Signs of Bullying in Everyday Relationships

Bullying doesn't only happen in workplaces — it can surface in friendships, families, and romantic relationships. It can wear the mask of love, loyalty, or humour, making it difficult to name. These behaviours are often excused as personality quirks or emotional "overreactions," yet they quietly corrode self-trust, dignity, and safety.

The following signs reflect patterns of relational bullying drawn from lived experience and survivor testimony.

• **Gaslighting:** Denying your reality, rewriting events, or making you feel irrational for expressing pain. Over time, this weakens your confidence in trusting your own perceptions.
• **Silent treatment:** Refusing to communicate as a means of punishment or control. What looks like "space" is often strategic withdrawal — a weaponised absence.
• **Passive-aggression:** Sarcasm, backhanded compliments, or subtle digs that undermine confidence. It leaves you apologising for wounds you didn't cause.
• **Emotional invalidation:** Dismissing your feelings, minimising

your hurt, or refusing to acknowledge harm. The message is clear: your pain is inconvenient.

• **Control disguised as care:** Dictating your choices under the guise of concern or protection. The bully hides behind "I'm just looking out for you" while erasing your autonomy.

• **Triangulation:** Involving third parties to manipulate, isolate, or create confusion. This keeps you off balance and competing for approval.

• **Jealousy masked as loyalty:** Resenting your growth, success, or connections while claiming to be protective. They want you small enough to manage.

• **Chronic criticism:** Constant fault-finding that chips away at confidence. The goal is not improvement — it's domination through erosion.

• **Conditional affection:** Offering love, support, or validation only when you comply. You learn that peace depends on surrender.

• **Boundary violations:** Ignoring your limits, mocking your boundaries, or punishing you for asserting yourself. To the bully, "no" is not a word — it's a challenge.

• **Public humiliation:** Subtle jabs or overt criticism delivered in front of others to assert control and diminish you socially.

• **Emotional withdrawal:** Withholding warmth, empathy, or intimacy as a form of punishment. Silence becomes a form of cruelty.

• **Deflection and blame-shifting:** Turning every confrontation into your fault. You end up apologising just to end the discomfort.

Relational bullying often hides behind charm, humour, or perceived closeness. Its tactics are psychological, but its damage is physical — fatigue, hypervigilance, and a nervous system constantly on alert.

Naming these patterns is the beginning of freedom. It restores language to what was blurred, meaning to what was twisted, and power to what was taken.

You do not owe kindness to cruelty or silence to survival. You owe yourself the truth — and the courage to walk away from anyone who cannot love without control.

Signs of Recovery and Reclamation

Healing is not linear. It moves in spirals — forward, backward, sideways — unfolding at the pace your nervous system can bear. Recovery does not mean forgetting what happened; it means remembering without losing yourself in the remembering.

The following signs reflect emotional, psychological, and relational shifts that often emerge as survivors begin to reclaim their voice, restore trust in their own perceptions, and rebuild a sense of safety in the world.

- **Clarity of thought:** Recognising patterns, naming harm, and trusting your own reality — even when others once denied it.
- **Emotional regulation:** Feeling deeply without being drowned by emotion. Allowing anger, grief, and joy to coexist without shame.
- **Boundary-setting:** Saying *no* without guilt, protecting your energy from manipulation, and refusing to shrink to make others comfortable.
- **Self-compassion:** Speaking to yourself with the tenderness you once gave to everyone else. Meeting your pain with patience instead of punishment.
- **Reconnection with joy:** Rediscovering what brings you peace,

laughter, and meaning — the simple acts that remind you of who you are beyond the harm.

• **Selective trust:** Choosing relationships that honour your truth, respect your limits, and reciprocate emotional labour.

• **Purposeful expression:** Transforming pain into power through art, writing, advocacy, or conversation. Speaking your story on your own terms.

• **Physical healing:** Noticing small returns of energy — steadier sleep, softer shoulders, calmer breath. The body remembering safety.

• **Spiritual anchoring:** Feeling reconnected to something greater — nature, creativity, community, faith, or the quiet wisdom within.

• **Legacy building:** Turning pain into purpose. Using what broke you to illuminate what endures. Becoming the person, you once needed.

Recovery is not about returning to who you were — it is about becoming who you were always meant to be: clear, grounded, and unshakably whole.

Closing Reflection

To those who have walked this path: you are not broken.

You are becoming.

This page has named what others deny, held space for truth, and honoured the quiet power of reclamation. It is not an ending — it is a threshold.

You have survived what was meant to silence you.

You have spoken what was meant to be buried.

You have chosen clarity over confusion, dignity over distortion, healing over harm.

Let this be your reminder: your story matters. Your voice is valid. Your legacy is unfolding in real time — in every act of courage, every boundary, every breath that says, *I am still here.*

When you are ready, turn the page.

Chapter 1 awaits — not as a beginning, but as a continuation of everything you have reclaimed.

You are here.

You are whole.

You are free.

PART I
Foundations of Harm and Clarity

When Silence Speaks First

I used to believe that truth would protect me.

That if I worked hard, stayed kind, and led with integrity, the system would respond in kind.

But the workplace wasn't built for truth. It was built for performance.

Smiles masked sabotage.

Meetings rehearsed manipulation.

The mask of professionalism was never meant to protect me — it was designed to erase me.

At first, I didn't notice. The signs were small, almost polite.

A meeting I wasn't invited to.

A project reassigned without explanation.

A colleague's sudden coldness after a private chat with management.

I told myself it was nothing — that I was imagining things.

That if I just worked harder, stayed humble, and kept my head down, the fog would lift.

But the fog wasn't mine.

It was theirs — a system designed to obscure, to confuse, to destabilise.

And so, I began to shrink — not because I lacked skill or heart,
but because I was being erased in slow motion.
My ideas were echoed without credit.
My presence was tolerated, not welcomed.
My instincts, once sharp and sure, began to doubt themselves.
This wasn't just a misunderstanding.
It was a recurring pattern.
A culture.
A reckoning waiting to be named.

PART I
The Dynamics of Workplace Bullying

Workplace bullying is not a single act — it is a system.

A culture.

A choreography of cruelty dressed in the costume of professionalism.

I once heard a line that stayed with me: *"The most dangerous people are those who believe they are virtuous while they destroy others."*

It named what I had lived.

In toxic workplaces, bullying is repackaged as "feedback," "team dynamics," or "performance management." Beneath the corporate language lies a darker truth — a deliberate erosion of dignity, clarity, and psychological safety.

These environments reward manipulation over merit. They elevate those who perform loyalty while punishing those who speak truth. The most dangerous players are often the most charming — masters of mimicry, deflection, and plausible deniability.

Bullying in these settings is rarely loud. It is quiet, strategic, cumulative:

• **Exclusion masked as oversight** — being left out of meetings, emails, or decisions.

• **Sabotage disguised as feedback** — undermining confidence under the guise of "development."
• **Isolation through triangulation** — turning colleagues against you with whispered half-truths.
• **Gaslighting as leadership** — rewriting events, denying harm, and making you doubt your own reality.

These tactics destabilise the target while preserving the illusion of professionalism. The system protects the abuser, not the abused.

What makes this dynamic so insidious is its ambiguity. There is rarely a smoking gun — only a slow corrosion of self-worth, clarity, and trust.

And when you finally speak up, the system responds not with care but with containment. HR becomes a shield for power. Colleagues fall silent. Leadership reframes your pain as "sensitivity."

This is not dysfunction.

It is design.

To name it is to reclaim your clarity.

To write it is to refuse erasure.

To speak it is to break the choreography.

This chapter is not just analysis.

It is testimony.

When Integrity Becomes a Threat

In toxic workplaces, integrity is not admired — it is feared.

Truth-tellers disrupt the choreography. Empaths expose the cruelty. High performers become targets not because they fail, but because they embody what the system cannot tolerate: clarity.

If you are emotionally intelligent, principled, and perceptive, you are dangerous to dysfunction. You see the patterns. You name the harm. You refuse to play the game.

And for that, you are punished.

You are excluded, undermined, reframed as *"difficult."*

Your strengths are twisted into flaws.

Your calm becomes "cold."

Your insight becomes "arrogance."

Your boundaries become "resistance."

This is not feedback.

It is erasure.

The System's Response to Truth

When you speak truth in a toxic workplace, the system does not listen — it defends itself.

You are met not with empathy but with containment. HR shields management. Colleagues look away. Leadership reframes your clarity as conflict, your boundaries as defiance.

The system does not want resolution; it wants silence.

You are offered mediation, not accountability.

You are told to "reflect," not to be heard.

You are urged to "move forward," while the harm remains unnamed.

This is not support.

It is suppression.

And when you refuse to be silenced, the system escalates.

You are isolated, performance-managed, or quietly erased.

Your reputation is rewritten.

Your legacy is redacted.

But here, in these pages, your truth remains.

Reclaiming the Narrative

To survive a toxic workplace is not merely to endure — it is to witness.

To name.

To reclaim.

You may leave with scars, but you also leave with sight.

You see the patterns.

You know the choreography.

You carry the truth.

And that truth is dangerous — not to you, but to the system that tried to erase you.

Reclamation begins when you stop asking for permission to be heard.

When you stop explaining your pain to those who benefit from your silence.

When you write, speak, and live as if your story matters — because it does.

This chapter does not end with resolution.

It ends with reclamation.

You are no longer asking the system to change.

You are changing the story.

PART II
Recovery Is Not Linear

Healing after workplace trauma is not a straight line.

It is a spiral — a reclamation — a quiet rebuilding of what was dismantled.

Some days you stand tall. Other days, a memory returns: a phrase, a glance, a meeting room that still hums in your nervous system.

Healing is not a race. It is a rhythm.

This Chapter Explores
- The emotional terrain of recovery
- The myths of "moving on"
- The tools of reclamation — boundaries, clarity, and self-trust

The Myth of Moving On

Society tells us to *move on.* To forgive. To forget. To reframe the pain as "growth."

But recovery is not forgetting — it is remembering with clarity.

It's about acknowledging what happened without hesitation.

It is refusing to gaslight yourself just because others did.

You don't have to stay silent for anyone.

You do not owe the system your compliance.

You owe yourself truth, care, and restoration.

Healing is not passive. It is not waiting for time to do the work.

It is active — boundary-setting, truth-telling, and choosing environments that honour your dignity.

You're not falling behind; you're building yourself back up.

The Nervous System Remembers

You may leave the building, but the building doesn't always leave you.

Your body remembers the hallway where you were humiliated.

The meeting room where your voice was dismissed.

The email tone that made your stomach drop.

These are not overreactions — they are echoes.

Trauma resides in the nervous system, not solely in the mind.

You may flinch at a calendar invite.

Feel dread before a Zoom call.

Freeze when someone says, *"Can I give you some feedback?"*

This isn't weakness; it's wisdom.

Your body is trying to protect you — to warn you, to remind you of what you survived.

Recovery begins when you listen — not to the system, but to yourself.

Boundaries as Medicine

After betrayal, boundaries are not just protective — they are medicinal.

They restore what was stolen: clarity, dignity, and choice.

You start saying *no* without feeling guilty.

You stop over-explaining.

You recognise that not every invitation is safe, and not every silence deserves interpretation.

Boundaries are not walls — they are doors.

They decide who enters, how long they stay, and what they bring with them.

You learn to trust your instincts again — the ones that warned you before the system gaslit them.

You stop asking, *"Was it really that bad?"* and start saying, *"I know what I felt."*

This is not bitterness.

It is healing.

Choosing Safety Over Approval

After betrayal, the hunger for approval begins to dissolve.

You realise that being liked is not the same as being safe.

That praise can coexist with sabotage.

That charm can mask cruelty.

You stop chasing validation from systems that harmed you.

You stop shrinking to fit into rooms that erased you.

You begin to ask a different question:

Not *"Do they like me?"*

But *"Do I feel safe?"*

Safety becomes your compass.

You choose environments that honour your boundaries, not just your skills.

You seek relationships that respect your truth, not just your performance.

This isn't selfishness; it's self-respect.

Final Reflection: The Slow Unlearning

It takes time to stop seeking approval — sometimes years, sometimes a lifetime.

We were taught that being liked meant being safe.

That praise meant belonging.

That silence meant peace.

But healing rewrites the script.

You begin to unlearn the reflex to please.

You stop contorting yourself to fit into spaces that never saw you.

You realise that approval is fleeting — but safety, clarity, and self-respect endure.

This unlearning is not failure.

It is return.

A slow, sacred return to yourself.

You are not too late.

You are right on time.

PART III
The Voice That Was Never Lost

You were never voiceless.

You were silenced.

There's a difference.

Your voice was always there — steady beneath the gaslighting, the exclusion, the performance reviews designed to confuse. It waited. It watched. It endured.

This chapter is about the return — the re-expression — the moment you stop whispering and start writing, speaking, creating.

It's not about revenge.

It's about restoration.

You do not need permission to tell your story.

You do not need approval to name what happened.

You do not need the system to validate your truth.

You are the witness.

The author.

The reckoning.

Creative Expression as Healing

When the system tries to erase you, creation becomes resistance.

Writing, painting, singing, speaking — these are not hobbies. They are reclamations. They are how you stitch yourself back together after being torn apart by silence.

You begin to write the words you were never allowed to say.

You create beauty from the wreckage.

You turn pain into poetry, silence into song, trauma into testimony.

Creative expression is not just catharsis — it is clarity. It is legacy.

You do not create to be understood by the system.

You create to be whole.

Every act of expression reclaims space that once belonged to fear. Every sentence, brushstroke, or melody is an act of defiance — and of healing.

Navigating Relationships After Betrayal

After betrayal, relationships become mirrors. Some reflect your healing. Others reflect your past.

You begin to notice who feels safe — and who feels familiar in the wrong way.

You stop mistaking intensity for intimacy.

You stop tolerating emotional shortcuts.

You learn to name your needs without apology.

You stop shrinking to preserve connection.

You stop explaining your boundaries to those who keep crossing them.

Some relationships deepen. Others dissolve.

This is not loss.

It is alignment.

You are no longer performing safety.

You are choosing it.

You begin to understand that your voice is not meant to convince — it is meant to *exist*.

You speak not for validation, but for freedom.

This chapter is not about rebuilding what was.

It is about creating what never was — spaces where your voice is heard, your truth is honoured, and your presence is wanted.

You are not finding your voice.

You are remembering it.

And this time, it answers only to you.

PART IV
The Anatomy of Betrayal

Betrayal is not always loud.
Sometimes it arrives in silence —
a meeting you weren't invited to,
a project reassigned without explanation,
a colleague's sudden shift in tone.
Beneath the surface, something fractures.
You realise the system was never neutral.
That the people you trusted were rehearsing your removal.
That your instincts were right — and that the gaslighting was not confusion, but design.
This chapter is about that moment —
the one where the mask slipped,
where you stopped doubting yourself and started naming the pattern.
It's not just about what happened.
It's about what it revealed.

Emotional Responses to Betrayal

Betrayal fractures more than trust — it fractures identity.

You may feel rage but have nowhere to place it.

You may feel grief but not know what you're mourning.

You might feel ashamed, even if you haven't done anything wrong.

These are not overreactions.

They are echoes of being erased.

You begin to question everything: your instincts, your worth, your memory.

You replay conversations, searching for the moment it turned.

You wonder if you imagined it — until the pattern confirms itself.

This isn't paranoia.

It's pattern recognition.

You have lived this.

You've walked into rooms where the lies arrived before you.

You've felt the sting of being shunned before you could speak.

You've grieved the loss of a career, a self, a future stolen in slow motion.

And still — you chose truth.

How Betrayal Reshapes Trust, Truth, and Legacy

After betrayal, trust becomes sacred. You no longer offer it freely. You observe. You discern. You listen not just to words, but to patterns.

Trust becomes a slow rebuild. You learn that not everyone who smiles is safe — and that distance can be an act of love for yourself. **Truth** becomes non-negotiable. You stop softening your story to protect others. You stop explaining your pain to those who benefit from your silence. You begin to speak with clarity, not permission. **Legacy** becomes urgent. You realise your story must be told — not only for yourself, but for those still being erased. You write not to be liked, but to be clear. You create not to be praised, but to be whole.

This is not bitterness.
It is sovereignty.
This chapter is not just about betrayal — it is about what betrayal reveals, and what it cannot destroy.
You were never without a voice.
You were made to be silent.
There's a difference.

Your voice was always there — steady beneath the gaslighting, the exclusion, the performance reviews designed to confuse. It waited. It watched. It endured.

This is the return.

The re-expression.

The moment you stop whispering and start writing, speaking, creating.

It's not about revenge.

It's about restoration.

You do not need permission to tell your story.

You do not need approval to name what happened.

You do not need the system to validate your truth.

You are the witness.

The author.

The reckoning.

PART V
The Psychology of Gaslighting

Gaslighting is not just lying.

It is strategic distortion — a deliberate attempt to make you doubt your memory, your instincts, your reality.

It begins subtly: a denial here, a contradiction there.

You raise a concern, and they say, *"That never happened."*

You share your discomfort, and they respond with, *"You're over-reacting."*

You name a pattern, and they say, *"You're imagining things."*

Over time, you begin to question yourself.

You replay conversations.

You apologise for things you didn't do.

You shrink — not because you're wrong, but because you've been made to feel unreliable.

This is not miscommunication.

It is manipulation.

Common Gaslighting Tactics

- **Denial of events:** "That never happened."
- **Reframing your emotions:** "You're too sensitive."
- **Contradicting your memory:** "You're remembering it wrong."
- **Minimising your experience:** "It wasn't that bad."
- **Projecting blame:** "You're the one causing problem."
- **Isolating you from allies:** "They agree with me, not you."

These tactics are not random. They are rehearsed. They are calculated to destabilise and control.

You've lived this.

You've been told your instincts were wrong, even when they were right.

You've been asked to *"reflect"* when the harm was never named.

You've been offered mediation instead of accountability.

And still — you chose clarity.

Rebuilding Trust in Your Own Perception

Recovery begins when you stop outsourcing your reality.

When you stop asking others to confirm what you already know.

When you start saying, *"I trust what I felt."*

You begin to see the choreography clearly — the denials, the deflections, the distortions.

You stop explaining your truth to those who are committed to misunderstanding it.

You learn to discern the difference between disagreement and deception.

This is not defiance.

It is healing.

You learn to trust your instincts again — the same ones that warned you before the system gaslit them.

You stop asking, *"Was it really that bad?"* and start declaring, *"I know what I felt."*

And then, you begin to create.

To write.

To speak.

Not to convince — but to reclaim.

Not to be validated — but to be whole.

This chapter is not just about gaslighting.

It is about the return to self-trust, self-truth, and emotional sovereignty.

It is the moment your reality stops being debated and starts being lived.

You were never confused.

You were being convinced to doubt what you already knew.

Now — you remember.

PART VI
Emotional Sovereignty

There comes a moment in recovery when you stop reacting — and start discerning.

You no longer explain your boundaries. You no longer soften your truth. You no longer perform safety to preserve connection.

This is **emotional sovereignty**: the ability to feel, name, and express without distortion. It is the return to self-trust — the quiet refusal to be reshaped by systems that punished your clarity.

You begin to notice the difference between being **liked** and being **safe**. Between being **praised** and being **respected**. Between being **tolerated** and being **wanted**.

You stop asking, *"How do I make them understand?"* and start asking, *"Do I feel whole here?"*

This isn't arrogance; it's alignment.

You've calibrated your voice in friendships marked by illness and invalidation. You've chosen compassion without self-erasure. You've learned that boundaries are not punishment — they are protection.

This chapter is about that return — the steady, powerful reclamation of emotional clarity.

The moment you stop dimming your light to soothe others, and start shining with discernment.

You are not too much.
You are simply no longer willing to be less.

The Myth of Being "Too Much"

You were never too much. You were just too clear for those committed to confusion.

In toxic systems, **clarity** is reframed as intensity. **Emotion** is reframed as instability. **Truth** is reframed as threat.

You are told to tone it down. To be more "professional." To smile more. To soften your words. To dilute your instincts.

But what they really mean is: *Be less of yourself so we can stay comfortable.*

You begin to internalise the myth. You apologise for your insight. You shrink your joy. You rehearse your truth in whispers.

Until one day, you stop.

You realise that being *"too much"* was never the problem.

The problem was being surrounded by people who preferred distortion over truth.

You've been called intense, difficult, even arrogant — not because you were wrong, but because you were clear.

You've chosen to keep shining, even when others flinch at your light.

This is not defiance.

It is dignity.

The Power of Emotional Boundaries

Emotional boundaries are not walls — they are clarity.

They define what you will hold, what you will release, and what you will no longer absorb.

You stop taking responsibility for other people's discomfort.

You stop translating your truth into a language that erases you.

You stop performing calm when your body is begging for honesty.

Boundaries are not cruelty. They are care — for yourself, and for the relationships that can hold truth.

You begin to say:
- "I won't explain my pain to those who caused it."
- "I won't soften my truth to preserve someone else's comfort."
- "I won't shrink to be palatable."

You've chosen emotional calibration over emotional erasure.

You've learned to attune without abandoning yourself.

You've practised truth not to provoke, but to protect.

This isn't detachment; it's discernment.

Final Reflection: The Return to Self

Emotional sovereignty is not a destination.
   It is a return.
   A return to the instincts once doubted.
   A return to the voice once silenced.
   A return to the self once reshaped to soothe others.
   You do not owe anyone your dilution.
   You don't owe anyone your silence.
   You do not owe anyone your disappearance.
   You are not too much.
   You are simply no longer willing to be less.
   This chapter closes not with resolution, but with reclamation.
   You are no longer performing safety.
   You are choosing it.

PART VII
Spiritual Anchoring

There comes a point in recovery when healing is no longer only emotional — it becomes spiritual.

You begin to ask different questions.

Not *"Why did they do this?"* but *"What did this bring out in me?"*

Not *"How do I fix this?"* but *"What do I carry forward?"*

Spiritual anchoring is not about bypassing pain. It is about naming it, holding it, and choosing to rise with it.

You begin to see the patterns not merely as cruelty, but as curriculum. You start to trust that your clarity is not only earned — it is sacred.

You've lived this. You've turned grief into wisdom. You've chosen dignity over despair. You've found meaning in the wreckage and purpose in the pain.

This chapter is not about religion. It is about reverence — for truth, for healing, for the soul that refused to be erased.

Legacy as Spiritual Practice

Legacy is not just what you leave behind. It is what you live by.

It is the truth you refuse to bury, the clarity you choose over comfort, the voice you honour even when others flinch.

After betrayal, legacy becomes sacred. You begin to write not to be liked, but to be clear. You begin to speak not to be praised, but to be whole. You begin to live not to perform, but to align.

This isn't just a book; it's a revelation. A mirror. A sanctuary. It carries the weight of what was lost — and the light of what was reclaimed.

This is not merely healing. It is devotion.

Final Reflection: Sacred Ground

Spiritual anchoring is not an escape. It is a grounding — a way of standing barefoot in the truth and saying, *"I am still here."*

You begin to see your story not as a wound, but as a well.

Not as a burden, but as a beacon.

Not as shame, but as scripture.

You stop asking for closure and start creating meaning.

Your clarity is sacred.

Your legacy is sacred.

Your refusal to be erased is sacred.

This is not just healing.

It is consecration.

PART II
Systems, Patterns, and Reform

PART VIII
The Systemic Mirror

Your betrayal was not an anomaly.

It was a reflection —

a reflection of systems that reward performance over integrity,

that punish clarity,

that rehearse harm while preaching inclusion.

This chapter is not about one manager, one meeting, or one moment.

It is about the choreography — the way cruelty is normalised, silence is incentivised, and truth is reframed as disruption.

You've seen this.

You've named it.

You've refused to be gaslit by the system that created the harm and then denied it.

This chapter explores:
• The cultural gaslighting of high performers
• The architecture of complicity
• How systems protect power, not people
• Why truth-tellers are reframed as threats

The Culture of Complicity

In toxic systems, silence is not neutral — it is participation.

Colleagues witness the harm but say nothing. Managers observe the sabotage and call it *"team dynamics."* HR hears the truth and rebrands it as *"a personality clash."*

This isn't oversight; it's orchestration.

Complicity is not just what people do — it's what they refuse to name:

the meeting where no one speaks up,

the email thread where truth is buried,

the performance review that punishes clarity.

You've lived this. You've watched people rehearse care while enabling cruelty. You've seen charm weaponised and professionalism used to erase.

This isn't dysfunction; it's intentional design.

The Gaslighting of High Performers

In toxic systems, high performers are not celebrated — they are destabilised.

You show up with clarity, integrity, and emotional intelligence. You name patterns. You ask questions. You refuse to play the game.

And for that, you are punished.

You are told you're *"Too intense," "too sensitive," "too much."*

Your strengths are reframed as liabilities.

Your insight is called arrogance.

Your boundaries are labelled resistance.

This is not feedback. It is gaslighting.

You've lived this. You've been asked to *"reflect"* when the harm was never named. You've been offered mediation instead of accountability. You've been recast as the problem — not because you were wrong, but because you were clear.

High performers threaten dysfunction. They see the choreography, name the harm, and refuse to be reshaped.

This isn't defiance; it's discernment.

The Architecture of Complicity

Complicity is not passive — it is structural.

It lives in performance reviews that punish truth, HR protocols that prioritise optics over accountability, and leadership models that reward charm over integrity.

The system is not broken. It is working exactly as designed: to protect power, obscure harm, and silence truth.

You raise a concern, and they offer mediation.

You name a pattern, and they call it *"a clash of personalities."*

You ask for accountability, and they recommend *"self-reflection."*

This isn't care; it's confinement.

You've seen policies used to deflect rather than defend, and empathy replaced with strategy. You've named the choreography — and refused to dance.

This isn't dysfunction; it's design.

How Systems Protect Power, Not People

Systems are not neutral. They are built to preserve hierarchy.

Policies deflect accountability. Protocols contain truth. Leadership structures reward loyalty over integrity.

You raise a concern, and they cite procedure.

You name harm, and they reference policy.

You ask for justice, and they offer optics.

This is not protection. It is preservation — of image, hierarchy, and control.

You've seen HR shield the abuser.

You've heard leadership reframe cruelty as *"miscommunication."*

You've been told to "move on" while the harm remains unnamed.

Systems do not protect the vulnerable. They protect the powerful.

This isn't an oversight; it's intentional architecture.

Why Truth-Tellers Are Reframed as Threats

Truth-tellers disrupt the choreography.

They name what others deny. They refuse to perform safety while harm is rehearsed.

In toxic systems, truth is not welcomed — it is reframed.

You speak up, and they call you *"difficult."*

You name a pattern, and they say you're *"overreacting."*

You set a boundary, and they label you *"not a team player."*

This is not misunderstanding. It is strategy.

You've been punished for clarity and reframed as the problem while the harm was preserved. You've watched the system respond to truth not with care, but with containment.

Truth-tellers are dangerous to dysfunction. They expose the choreography, threaten the illusion, and refuse to be reshaped.

This isn't defiance; it's integrity.

Final Reflection: The Mirror That Doesn't Lie

Systems may distort, but the mirror doesn't lie.

You saw the choreography. You named the harm. You refused to be reshaped.

You were called difficult, intense, arrogant — not because you were wrong, but because you were clear.

You stopped asking for permission. You stopped performing safety. You stopped translating your truth into a language that erased you.

You've walked through the fire of betrayal and emerged with clarity. You've chosen legacy over silence. You've held the mirror to the system — and refused to look away.

This is not rebellion. It is reckoning.

This is not the end of the chapter. This is the start of the truth.

PART IX
Generational Impact

Some betrayals do not end with the individual.

They echo.

They echo in the nervous systems of children who watched their parents shrink.

They echo in the career choices of those who learned that safety mattered more than truth.

They echo in the silence passed down like heirlooms.

This chapter is not just about what happened to you.

It is about what happens next — in families, in communities, in legacies.

You've lived this. You've felt the grief not only for yourself, but for what could have been — the generational potential lost to cruelty, the emotional intimacy stolen by sabotage, the legacy interrupted.

This chapter explores:
• How betrayal shapes generational patterns
• The grief of lost potential
• The inheritance of silence and fear
• How truth-telling becomes legacy

The Inheritance of Silence and Fear

Silence is not only a response. It is a legacy.

Children learn to shrink by watching their parents punished for truth.

Colleagues learn to stay quiet by watching whistle-blowers erased.

Communities learn to perform safety by watching harm go unnamed.

This is not just trauma. It is transmission.

Fear becomes inherited — not through genetics, but through example.

Through the stories that were never told.

Through the truths that were buried to survive.

You've felt this weight — the quiet burden of unspoken pain.

But you've also chosen to break the pattern: not out of rebellion, but restoration.

You speak not only for yourself, but for every voice that was silenced before yours.

This isn't rebellion; it's reclamation.

How Truth-Telling Becomes Legacy

Legacy is not only what you leave behind.

It is what you refuse to bury.

When you name the harm, you break the silence.

When you write the story, you interrupt the transmission.

When you speak the truth, you change the inheritance.

This is not merely healing.

It is legacy-building.

You've chosen this path deliberately — to survive, to consecrate, to transform betrayal into blueprint.

You've chosen to leave behind clarity, not confusion; truth, not tolerance; courage, not compliance.

Your truth is not just yours.

It is a gift to those who come after.

Final Reflection: The Grief and the Gift

Some truths arrive as grief. Others arrive as gift.

Yours arrived as both.

You grieve the career that could have flourished, the relationships that could have deepened, the legacy that could have expanded.

Yet you also carry the gift — of clarity, of courage, of consecration.

You write not only to heal, but to interrupt the transmission.

You speak not only for yourself, but for those who were silenced.

You leave behind not only insight, but inheritance.

This is not merely a book.

It is a legacy. A reckoning. A restoration.

PART III
Psychological Insight and Recovery

Final Therapist's Note: Why Certain People Are Targeted – and How to Break the Cycle

People are often targeted by narcissists and bullies not because they are weak, but because they possess qualities that threaten or expose the insecurities of the perpetrator.

Empathy, integrity, and authenticity shine a light that manipulative personalities cannot tolerate.

Narcissists and bullies operate from insecurity, envy, and control-seeking. Their behaviour is often driven by:

• **Fear of exposure:** they target those whose competence and ethics reveal their own inadequacy.
• **Need for dominance:** they seek to control environments and will undermine anyone who resists or outshines them.
• **Projection and deflection:** by attacking others, they avoid facing their own flaws.

Who Is Targeted — and Why

Empaths and Highly Sensitive People
• Deeply attuned to others' emotions, they extend benefit of the doubt.

• Their compassion can be exploited by those who manipulate guilt or obligation.

Competent and Ethical Individuals
• Integrity threatens those who rely on deception or shortcuts.
• Competence exposes the inadequacy of narcissistic or territorial colleagues.

Survivors of Past Abuse
• Narcissists often "test" boundaries early, sensing unresolved trauma.
• Conditioned tolerance of mistreatment can delay recognition until patterns repeat.

People with Low Assertiveness or High Agreeableness
• Those who avoid conflict or over-prioritise harmony may not push back immediately.
• Bullies interpret this restraint as permission to escalate.

Why It Happens Repeatedly
This pattern persists when environments and inner narratives remain unhealed:

• **Unconscious signalling:** survivors may display hyper-vigilance or over-accommodation — cues predators' exploit.
• **Lack of systemic accountability:** toxic individuals flourish where leadership fails to intervene.
• **Internalised doubt:** repeated undermining makes survivors question their own perceptions.

Breaking the cycle requires both personal and structural repair: trauma-informed therapy, assertiveness training, supportive networks, and workplaces with genuine accountability.

Why Narcissists, Sociopaths, and Workplace Psychopaths Seem Popular

They appear popular because they are masters of performance, manipulation, and strategic charm — especially in curated spaces like social media and hierarchical organisations.

1. Charm as a Tactical Tool
• Possess high social intelligence but limited empathy.
• Read rooms astutely, mirror desires, and project confidence.
• Crave admiration and manufacture likability to secure power.

2. Curated Personas and Social Media Illusions
• Platforms reward image over substance.
• Narcissistic personalities excel at constructing idealised versions of success and desirability.
• Algorithms amplify visibility, creating feedback loops that glorify manipulation.

3. Manipulative Relationship Strategies
• Relationships are transactional — allies, admirers, or enablers serve their agenda.
• The appearance of popularity masks emotional shallowness.

4. Social Proof and Fear of Missing Out
• Popularity reinforces itself.
• People conflate admiration with value, mistaking charisma for character.

5. The Illusion of Connection
• Their "friends" are often surface-level contacts sustained by performance, not vulnerability.
• The illusion of warmth conceals an aversion to accountability.

Closing Reflection
Understanding why you were targeted is not about blame — it is about liberation.

Your empathy was never the problem. Your integrity was never the weakness.

You were chosen because you carried light into a room built to hide shadows.

To break the cycle is to see the pattern, name it, and step out of its choreography.

That choice — your choice — becomes the legacy that ends the echo.

Vignette 1: The Illusion of Popularity

Client: *Maya, 42 — Graphic Designer*

Presenting Issues: Chronic anxiety, self-doubt, and workplace burnout

Context:
Maya worked under Ethan; a senior manager widely admired across the company. His social media glowed with motivational quotes, team selfies, and endless streams of heart emojis. In the office, he was charismatic, articulate, and perpetually "on." To everyone watching, he embodied leadership, charm, and success.
Behind closed doors, the narrative took a different turn.

Therapeutic Unfolding:
Maya described feeling increasingly confused and isolated. Ethan publicly praised her contributions — then privately took credit for her ideas, gaslit her about deadlines, and excluded her from key meetings.
When she tried to raise her concerns, colleagues dismissed her: "But Ethan's amazing! Look how many people adore him."

Each dismissal deepened her doubt. Gratitude turned into guilt. Competence turned into shame. She began apologising for simply existing in rooms where her truth was inconvenient. The pressure eroded her confidence, and her body began to protest: insomnia, digestive issues, panic attacks that made her fear her own success.

Therapeutic Insight:
Through trauma-informed therapy, Maya began to see what had been hidden in plain sight: Ethan's popularity was not proof of virtue — it was performance. His charm was a mask, his praise a manipulation, his "friendships" a network of strategic alliances. The likes, comments, and admiration were not reflections of character, but echoes of a curated persona.
Once Maya could name the pattern, clarity returned. She began documenting his behaviour, reclaiming her narrative, and disentangling her worth from his projection. Eventually, she transitioned to a workplace where integrity mattered more than image.

Resolution:
Maya now advocates for psychological safety in creative industries. She teaches others how to discern genuine connection from performative charisma — reminding survivors that popularity does not equal empathy, and visibility does not equal virtue.
Her story reveals a vital truth:
Some of the most dangerous abusers are the ones everyone loves.

Vignette 2: The Social Media Darling

Client: *Jasmine, 29 — Yoga Instructor*

Presenting Issues: Emotional exhaustion, fear of confrontation, loss of self-trust

Context:
Jasmine admired Lena, a wellness influencer with thousands of followers. Lena's feed overflowed with affirmations, sunset meditations, and photos of her "tribe" — all soft smiles, retreats, and heart emojis.
When they met at a local event, Jasmine felt instantly seen. Lena praised her online, reposted her content, and invited her to collaborate on classes and retreats. The attention felt validating — like a door opening to possibility.
But behind the filtered glow, something darker stirred.

Therapeutic Unfolding:
Lena's charm turned conditional. She began dictating what Jasmine should post, criticising her tone and even her body under the guise

of "brand alignment." She mocked Jasmine privately, claiming to be "helping her grow."

When Jasmine tried to set boundaries, Lena withdrew her affection like a weapon.

She unfollowed her, deleted their collaborations, and quietly rallied mutual followers with posts about "betrayal" and "protecting her energy."

Jasmine was left isolated and confused — watching her reputation wither while Lena's influence bloomed. Every double-tap and hashtag felt like proof that Lena was right, and Jasmine was not enough.

Her nervous system began to echo the manipulation: sleepless nights, racing thoughts, a shrinking sense of self.

Therapeutic Insight:
Through trauma-informed therapy, Jasmine began to see through the illusion.

Lena's social media presence was not authenticity — it was architecture. A curated façade of virtue and vulnerability used to mask control and extract validation. The heart emojis were not evidence of empathy — they were tools of influence.

Lena had used spiritual language to justify cruelty, calling manipulation "boundaries" and abandonment "healing." Her so-called "tribe" was a revolving door of people temporarily useful to her image.

As Jasmine named these patterns, clarity returned. She rebuilt her voice and her online presence from a place of integrity, not imitation. Her work now centres on **authentic wellness** — where spirituality heals rather than hides harm.

Resolution:
Jasmine now teaches others how to recognise *spiritual bypassing, performative empathy*, and *image-based intimacy*.

Her story is a reminder that influence is not the same as integrity — and that true healing cannot coexist with manipulation disguised as light.

Sometimes the brightest feeds hide the darkest lessons.

Vignette 3: The Family Favourite

Client: *Daniel, 36 — School Teacher*

Presenting Issues: Depression, people-pleasing, unresolved childhood trauma

Context:
Daniel grew up in the shadow of his older brother, Mark — the golden child.
Mark was charming, athletic, and effortlessly adored by the extended family. At every gathering, he commanded attention. His jokes drew laughter, his stories drew admiration, and his every achievement was celebrated as proof of family pride.
Behind closed doors, the dynamic was far less golden.
Mark belittled Daniel, mocked his sensitivity, and manipulated their parents to his advantage. When Daniel tried to speak up, the family's response was swift and silencing:
"You're too sensitive."
"You're just jealous."
Over time, Daniel learned that silence kept the peace. He became

the peacemaker, the helper, the invisible one. He performed niceness to earn belonging and buried his truth to avoid conflict.

Therapeutic Unfolding:
In therapy, Daniel began to name what had always been unnamed: Mark's popularity was performance, not purity. His charm was a form of control, his laughter a mask. The family's admiration was not evidence of goodness — it was a collective denial of emotional truth. As Daniel peeled back the layers, grief surfaced — grief for the childhood safety he never had, and for the adult years spent contorting himself to stay lovable. He began validating his own reality, recognising that the role he played — the quiet, compliant one — was a survival strategy, not his identity.
Setting boundaries was not easy. Family members resisted, some retreating into silence or defensiveness. But Daniel stood firm. He learned that peace born of suppression is not peace at all — it is self-erasure.

Resolution:
Daniel now teaches emotional literacy to his students and models healthy boundaries in his own relationships. He has stopped trying to earn love through compliance and begun cultivating connection through authenticity.
His healing marks a generational turning point — a quiet revolution against the inheritance of silence.
Sometimes the family favourite is simply the one who never challenged the lie.
And sometimes healing means daring to tell the truth anyway.

Breaking the Cycle
Therapeutic recovery from family-based emotional abuse involves:
• **Naming the pattern** — recognising manipulation, favouritism, and the tactics that maintain control.
• **Reclaiming boundaries** — practising assertiveness and emotional detachment from toxic dynamics.

• **Reframing identity** — understanding that being targeted or dismissed is not a flaw, but often a reflection of one's light in the presence of another's shadow.

Healing in this context is not rebellion.
It is self-respect.
It is the reclamation of truth over tradition.

PART IV
Scenes from the Reckoning

Each story is not merely an account—it is evidence. Evidence of systems that harm, betray, and erase. But it is also testimony: a record of courage, clarity, and reclamation.

These aren't just stories; they're evidence.

Evidence of sabotage disguised as strategy.

Of cruelty rehearsed as care.

Of betrayal performed in public spaces.

Each scene is a mirror.

Each moment, a reckoning.

You've lived these. You've carried them in silence.

Now, you name them — not for revenge, but for restoration.

This is not indulgence.

It is testimony.

Case Study: Caroline

Background

Caroline, a 24-year-old administration officer, joined a cohesive and well-regarded team at a local hospital. Her role included rotating shifts, managing financial reconciliation, and overseeing the mail ledger. The group was known for its professionalism and camaraderie.

Incident Overview

The culture changed dramatically when a new part-time employee, Delilah, joined the team. Though outwardly friendly, Delilah expressed a desire for full-time work, once remarking ominously, *"Someone always leaves, eventually."* Her behaviour soon disrupted the workplace harmony and centred on undermining Caroline.

"Just once in my life, I'd actually
like to see liar's pants catch on fire"
– Veronica Ruff

REACTIVE ABUSE

"People will provoke you
until they get a reaction,
then call you crazy
for responding."

– Veronica Ruff

Key Incidents

- **False Attribution and Undermining:** Delilah made repeated financial errors. When Caroline offered to help, Delilah later accused her of being critical and aggressive.
- **Manipulation and Isolation:** Delilah ingratiated herself with management while quietly discrediting Caroline's professionalism.
- **Sabotage:** Caroline's keys disappeared during a shared shift and were later found positioned to fall into a mailbag.
- **Verbal and Physical Intimidation:** Delilah shouted over Caroline's calls, then threw folders at her when alone.
- **Emotional Abuse:** Delilah mocked Caroline's recent breakup, implying she was unlovable.
- **Public Shaming and Gaslighting:** Other staff began to avoid Caroline, influenced by Delilah's narrative.

Impact on the Victim

Caroline experienced emotional devastation, confusion, and severe stress reactions, including insomnia, crying spells, and somatic symptoms. She ultimately resigned mid-shift, overwhelmed and afraid.

Therapeutic and Legal Analysis

Delilah's actions meet Safe Work Australia's definition of workplace bullying — repeated, unreasonable behaviour creating risk to health and safety. Caroline's withdrawal and emotional collapse align with trauma exposure and psychological injury.

Protective Framing for Publication

All names and identifiers have been changed. No formal allegation of underperformance was made by Caroline. The described incidents are documented recollections and should be read as lived experience, not legal adjudication.

Professional Commentary

Caroline's experience demonstrates the damage of covert bullying and organisational denial. The manipulator's charm, combined with managerial inaction, created an unsafe environment that eroded trust and wellbeing. Her story is not just a warning — it is a call for trauma-informed leadership and systemic accountability.

Transition

Caroline's story reveals how cruelty can hide in plain sight — how silence, charm, and policy can merge into a quiet violence that leaves lasting scars. But she was not alone. In another hospital, under a different roof but within the same broken architecture, another woman faced the same choreography — performed by different actors, sustained by the same system.

INTERLUDE: **From Evidence to Reform**

Caroline's story is not an outlier.

It is a pattern.

Across industries, sectors, and institutions, the choreography repeats itself — charm before cruelty, performance before punishment, silence before collapse.

Different workplaces.

Same architecture.

The reckoning begins when these stories are placed side by side. When the "isolated incidents" start to sound identical. When the harm is no longer individual, but systemic.

These pages are not about revenge or ruin. They are about revelation.

They document what happens when human dignity collides with unchecked power — and what emerges when the truth is finally named.

In the chapters that follow, we will trace these patterns across fields and functions.

We will examine how language, policy, and hierarchy can be weaponised to conceal abuse.

We will look at how organisations rewrite harm as "conflict," and why truth-tellers so often become exiles.

But we will also turn toward reform.

Toward frameworks of accountability.

Toward cultures where care is not performative — it is policy.

This is the threshold between evidence and evolution.

Between surviving the system and transforming it.

Between silence and systemic change.

You've named the harm.

Now we name what must come next.

WHEN PEOPLE TREAT YOU DISRESPECTFULLY

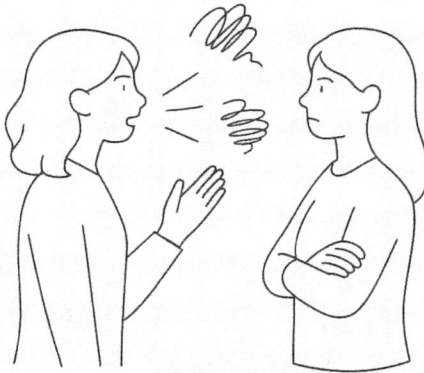

"Kindness is sacred —
but it must be protected."

— Veronica Ruff

DELIBERATE HARM

"Some harm isn't accidental.
They knew what they
were doing —
and you remember
every smirk.

Case Study: Candace

THE SCAPEGOAT

Background

Candace began work as a front-line reception and administration officer at a local hospital. Her role involved switchboard operations, patient liaison, and after-hours coordination with mental health teams. From the first week, she sensed dysfunction — a culture of avoidance, blame, and fear.

Incident Overview

Candace became the scapegoat for systemic failures. Managers, clinical staff, and administrative teams repeatedly deflected accountability, leaving her exposed to humiliation, harassment, and danger.

Key Incidents

Mental Health Team Deflection: After following protocol during a patient self-harm crisis, Candace was wrongly blamed for the incident.

Public Humiliation: A registrar berated her in front of others for paging him during a cardiac arrest.

Threat from Patient's Husband: She received verbal threats after staff misdirected a visitor and shifted the blame to her.

Sexual Harassment: A contractor physically grabbed her; security intervened, but no follow-up support was offered.

Assault by a Nursing Unit Manager: Colleen, an Acting NUM, screamed and shoved Candace over a misdirected call.

Toilet Monitoring Petition: Colleagues timed Candace's toilet breaks and posted the log publicly.

Ministerial Complaint Setup: A fabricated complaint falsely accused Candace of neglecting a patient's family.

Administrative Chaos: When another department relocated without notice, she bore the brunt of angry calls and confusion.

Public Humiliation at Team Building: In the final act of cruelty, an administrative staff member told her that she had been there too long and that it was time for her to "move on" in front of peers.

Impact on the Victim
Candace experienced severe emotional distress, anxiety, nightmares, and physical illness. She reported feelings of isolation, loss of confidence, and financial stress from payroll errors.

Therapeutic and Legal Analysis
These actions constitute repeated, unreasonable behaviour creating risk to health and safety. The workplace's failure to intervene breached its duty of care. Patterns of narcissistic manipulation, group bullying, and public shaming were evident.

Protective Framing for Publication
This case is presented with factual integrity and legal caution:

- No formal misconduct findings were recorded against individuals.
- The contractor's removal followed Candace's report.
- The "toilet petition" was witnessed but never formally acknowledged.
- All names and identifying details have been altered.

Professional Commentary

Candace's case exposes the intersection of negligence and cruelty in healthcare settings. Her experience demonstrates how vulnerable workers — particularly women in front-line roles — can be targeted by systems that protect image over integrity. Her departure was not a failure; it was an act of self-preservation. Candace's story calls for urgent reform: trauma-informed leadership, safe reporting mechanisms, and a culture that values wellbeing over optics.

Closing Reflection

Each of these stories carries a common thread: it was never about one person. It was about a system built to protect power. Caroline's silence and Candace's scapegoating reveal what happens when truth is treated as a threat, and harm is dressed as professionalism. They survived what the system tried to bury. And by naming it, they begin to unearth us all.

Case Study: Breanne

THE PROFESSIONAL UNDERMINED

Background

After a long and successful career in the IVF sector, Breanne chose to transition into a slower-paced administrative role at a public health clinic. Her decision was deeply intentional — a move toward balance, family, and wellbeing over title or prestige. The new position offered regular hours and proximity to her children's school, allowing her to participate in everyday family life again — school runs, assemblies, and sports days. For the first time in years, she felt she might find professional peace.

Incident Overview

That peace was short-lived. From her first day, Breanne was subjected to sustained undermining, exclusion, and subtle hostility by a colleague named Rachel — an employee whose behaviour had reportedly driven several staff members to resign before her arrival.

Despite Breanne's professionalism, calm demeanour, and willingness to contribute, Rachel's actions poisoned the environment and ultimately forced Breanne to leave the clinic she had once hoped would be her sanctuary.

Key Incidents

Hostile Welcome: On Breanne's first day, Rachel arrived late, assessed her attire, and remarked with thinly veiled sarcasm, "We don't usually dress up like that here."
Why it occurred: Rachel perceived Breanne's composure and professionalism as a threat to her own status and responded with territorial aggression masked as humour.

Sabotage by Technology: Rachel frequently disrupted Breanne's work by controlling the shared printer — turning it off remotely, removing paper, and interrupting critical printing tasks.
Why it occurred: Intentional obstruction designed to frustrate Breanne and assert control over shared resources.

Strategic Exclusion: When the clinic arranged transport for a professional forum, Rachel intentionally omitted Breanne from the list. Later, she laughed and said, "Oh — I guess you'll have to miss it."
Why it occurred: A deliberate attempt to isolate Breanne, diminish her visibility, and undermine her professional credibility.

Impact on the Victim
The cumulative effect of Rachel's conduct was profound. Breanne experienced:

- Emotional exhaustion and disillusionment
- Professional embarrassment and self-doubt
- Loss of trust in leadership due to silence and inaction
- Withdrawal from a role that had once represented stability and belonging

Breanne's resignation was not a failure — it was a survival decision.

Therapeutic and Legal Analysis
Rachel's conduct meets Safe Work Australia's definition of

workplace bullying: repeated, unreasonable behaviour that creates a risk to health and safety. Breanne's case involved:

- Psychological undermining through exclusion and ridicule
- Task sabotage designed to erode performance confidence
- Passive-aggressive hostility framed as workplace banter

Management's failure to intervene despite observable behaviour perpetuated the harm and eroded Breanne's psychological safety. Her decision to transfer to the casual staffing pool was a trauma-informed act of self-preservation — reclaiming autonomy and distance from toxicity.

Protective Framing for Publication

- This case study reflects Breanne's lived experience, presented with transparency and legal caution:
- Rachel's behaviour was observed by colleagues and addressed by the Nursing Unit Manager.
- No formal disciplinary action was recorded.
- Breanne's resignation was voluntary following repeated incidents of distress.
- Rachel was subsequently relocated and no longer works at the clinic in question.
- All names and identifying details have been altered.

Professional Commentary

Breanne's experience exemplifies how micro-level sabotage — subtle exclusions, ridicule, and professional obstruction — can inflict deep psychological injury over time. Her story is a reminder that bullying does not always involve shouting or overt aggression; sometimes, it is the quiet manipulation of systems, relationships, and opportunities.

Early intervention is critical. Leadership silence is not neutrality — it is complicity. The clinic's failure to protect Breanne reinforced a

toxic culture and cost the organisation a capable, ethical professional. Breanne's decision to walk away was not weakness. It was
wisdom — an act of reclamation and a refusal to let cruelty define
her worth.

Her story stands as both a warning and a testament: dignity must
never be sacrificed for stability, and peace is found not in compliance, but in clarity.

Case Study: Shirley

THE WORKPLACE NARCISSIST

Background

After years working in uniformed service, Elena accepted a front-line reception role at a prestigious government department. The position offered excellent pay, a nine-day fortnight, and the stability she needed to prioritise her family.

For Elena, this was more than a job — it was a fresh start. She looked forward to returning to a professional environment, wearing corporate attire, and contributing meaningfully in a role that aligned with her values and experience.

But beneath the department's polished image, a corrosive dynamic was already at play.

Incident Overview

From the outset, Elena became the target of sustained psychological manipulation by her colleague, Shirley — a long-serving employee whose influence in the department masked a pattern of intimidation and deceit.

What began as subtle undermining soon escalated into deliberate sabotage, fraud, and emotional abuse. Despite Elena's professionalism and resilience, the environment became intolerable, culminating in psychological injury and eventual reassignment.

Key Incidents

Hostile Welcome: On Elena's first day, Shirley arrived late, looked her over, and remarked that her attire was "a bit much for this place." She later monopolised the security staff and began imitating Elena's professional presentation while excluding her socially.
Why it occurred: Shirley perceived Elena's competence, poise, and confidence as a threat to her own fragile sense of superiority.

Sabotage of Resources: On a day when Shirley called in sick, Elena's essential "work bible" — a folder containing critical operational instructions — mysteriously disappeared. It was later found misplaced in a secure area only accessible to staff.
Why it occurred: Likely a calculated act to publicly undermine Elena's reliability and damage her reputation with management.

Email Fraud and Psychological Manipulation: Shirley gained unauthorised access to Elena's workstation and sent an offensive email from her account. The message violated departmental policy and initially appeared to implicate Elena.
Why it occurred: A manipulative attempt to discredit Elena and isolate her through manufactured scandal.

Social Sabotage and Reputation Damage: Shirley mirrored Elena's tone with senior executives, then began spreading rumours that Elena was "overly ambitious" and "trying to impress the boss." Colleagues began to withdraw.
Why it occurred: A classic triangulation tactic — fostering division to maintain control and dominance.

Escalation and Psychological Harm: The stress of ongoing manipulation led to panic attacks, nausea, and sleeplessness. Elena began to fear attending work.
Why it occurred: Chronic psychological abuse eroded Elena's sense of safety, triggering trauma responses.

Disclosure and Retaliation: Elena finally reported the harassment to the Executive Director, Tim, who investigated and promoted her to a new position. Shirley retaliated, demanding that Elena relieve her for breaks and sending a friend to monitor her movements.
Why it occurred: Shirley's narcissistic injury — the exposure of her manipulation — fuelled vindictive attempts to reassert control.

Timesheet Fraud and Final Reckoning: Tim later uncovered falsified timesheets submitted by Shirley and issued a department-wide directive reinforcing compliance. Shirley reacted with rage, accused Tim of misconduct, and attempted to rally others to her cause.
Why it occurred: The exposure of her deception shattered Shirley's curated image of competence and control.

Impact on the Victim
Elena's experience led to:

- Severe anxiety, panic attacks, and hypervigilance
- Reputational damage and professional isolation
- Loss of trust in leadership and peers
- Persistent trauma symptoms triggered by workplace settings
- Her recovery required months of therapy and a significant career shift. What had begun as a promising opportunity ended in profound psychological harm.

Therapeutic and Legal Analysis
Shirley's conduct meets Safe Work Australia's criteria for workplace

bullying and psychological harassment: repeated, unreasonable behaviour that creates a risk to health and safety.

Elena's experience involved:

- Fraudulent impersonation and reputational sabotage
- Triangulation and emotional manipulation
- Organisational neglect and delayed intervention
- While Tim's eventual action was instrumental in halting Shirley's misconduct, the department's earlier inaction allowed harm to escalate. Elena's reassignment provided safety, but the trauma's imprint remains — a testament to the deep psychological cost of systemic failure.

Protective Framing for Publication

This case study is based on Elena's verified experience. To ensure legal and ethical transparency:

- Multiple staff members corroborated Shirley's conduct.
- No formal charges were filed.
- Elena's promotion followed disclosure of the bullying.
- Shirley's eventual departure was not publicly linked to disciplinary findings.
- All names, identifying details, and institutional references have been altered for confidentiality.

Professional Commentary

Elena's story illustrates the devastating reality of workplace narcissism — where charisma, manipulation, and deceit are weaponised to control perception and eliminate perceived threats.

Her courage in reporting the abuse demonstrates both the cost and necessity of truth-telling in environments that prize image over integrity.

This case underscores a critical truth: leadership silence is not impartial — it is permissive. Without trauma-informed intervention, narcissistic abuse festers unchecked, eroding trust, morale, and mental health.

Elena's recovery is not defined by escape but by reclamation — of voice, dignity, and agency. Her testimony stands as a warning and a call to reform: when systems protect charm over truth, harm becomes culture.

Case Study: Susan

THE DYSFUNCTIONAL WORKPLACE

Background

Susan joined a community mental health clinic expecting professionalism, teamwork, and a shared commitment to client wellbeing. Instead, she entered a workplace defined by secrecy, instability, and psychological manipulation.

Several staff members with unresolved mental health challenges were tasked with supporting vulnerable clients — creating a volatile and unsafe environment where dysfunction was normalised.

Incident Overview

Over an 18-month period, Susan endured sustained bullying, racial targeting, and systemic neglect from multiple staff members, including her director and supervisor. What began as subtle exclusion escalated into coordinated sabotage, reputational destruction, and psychological injury that ultimately forced her resignation.

Key Incidents

Omission of Critical Information: Susan was never informed that all staff had lived experience of mental illness — a fact that profoundly shaped workplace culture and dynamics. She was left to navigate complex, emotionally charged interactions without context or support.

Why it occurred: A lack of transparency and disregard for psychological safety.

Sabotage and Role Manipulation: Joan repeatedly changed Susan's duties without notice, reassigned her tasks arbitrarily, and sent her on unnecessary errands under false pretences.

Why it occurred: To assert control and destabilise Susan's confidence.

Emergency Neglect and Staff Apathy: During multiple patient crises — including an overdose and a violent outburst — Susan was left to manage emergencies alone.

Why it occurred: Chronic mismanagement and systemic indifference to risk and accountability.

Equipment Theft and System Access Denial: A counsellor refused to return Susan's work laptop, leaving her unable to access essential systems during mandated remote work.

Why it occurred: Deliberate sabotage and managerial favouritism.

Racial Targeting and Narcissistic Abuse: Tonka publicly berated Susan, rallied staff against her, and filed a grievance to pre-empt accountability. When Susan lodged her own complaint, it was ignored. Tonka later stalked and verbally abused Susan in public.

Why it occurred: Narcissistic targeting reinforced by racial bias and institutional protection, due to Tonka's being a diversity, equity, and inclusion hire with lived mental health concerns.

Reputation Destruction and Forced Resignation: Tonka's harassment followed Susan into her next workplace. A fabricated complaint led to disciplinary proceedings, prompting Susan's immediate resignation.

Why it occurred: Continued targeting and unchecked reputational sabotage.

Impact on the Victim
Susan experienced:

- Severe anxiety, panic attacks, and physical illness
- Long-term loss of professional identity and trust
- Reputational damage extending across workplaces
- Ongoing fear of retaliation and job insecurity

Therapeutic and Legal Analysis
Susan's experience meets Safe Work Australia's definition of workplace bullying — repeated, unreasonable behaviour creating risk to health and safety.
Key elements include:

- Racial discrimination and public harassment
- Deliberate sabotage and exclusion from essential resources
- Organisational failure to provide psychological safety
- From a therapeutic perspective, Susan displayed trauma responses consistent with prolonged exposure to systemic abuse, including hypervigilance, withdrawal, and loss of professional confidence. The clinic's leadership breached its duty of care by ignoring warning signs and failing to intervene.

Protective Framing for Publication
This case study reflects Susan's lived experience and is presented with care to protect against defamation:

- No formal misconduct findings were issued against any individual.

- Events are described from the victim's documented perspective.
- Names, positions, and identifying details have been altered or fictionalised.
- The public incident described as harassment was non-physical but psychologically distressing.

Professional Commentary

Susan's story reveals the devastating cost of dysfunction in care settings. When leadership fails to uphold boundaries or provide trauma-informed oversight, workplaces meant for healing can become sites of harm.

Her experience underscores the urgent need for:

- Transparent recruitment and supervision practices
- Leadership training in psychological safety and anti-racism
- Accountability mechanisms that prioritise wellbeing over reputation

Susan's courage in naming what occurred transforms private pain into public insight. Her testimony is not merely personal — it is systemic evidence, calling institutions to confront the culture of silence that enables harm.

Interlude: From Personal Pathology to Systemic Failure

The stories so far have traced the anatomy of harm — how manipulation hides behind charm, how narcissism thrives in silence, and how good people are broken by systems that reward cruelty over conscience.

But sometimes, the damage isn't the work of one abuser. Sometimes, it's the system itself.

A culture so unwell that it mirrors the very disorders it claims to treat.

A workplace so steeped in dysfunction that neglect becomes normal, and trauma becomes policy.

The next case, *Susan — The Dysfunctional Workplace*, moves beyond the individual perpetrator. It examines what happens when leadership fails, accountability collapses, and institutions built to heal instead become engines of harm.

These are not anomalies. They are warnings.

Case Study: Karla

THE ILLUSION OF OPPORTUNITY AND PSYCHOLOGICAL INJURY

Background

Karla accepted a supervisory role at a private IVF clinic, believing it to be a pivotal career opportunity. The position offered strong remuneration and oversight of reception and switchboard operations. What she didn't know was that her appointment followed a quiet round of redundancies — displaced staff had been reassigned out of sight, and her new team had not been informed she was their supervisor.

Incident Overview

From her first day, Karla encountered resistance, exclusion, and subtle hostility. Her authority was undermined, her wellbeing deteriorated, and she was scapegoated for systemic dysfunction. Despite her efforts to implement structure and support, leadership failed to intervene, allowing bullying and sabotage to escalate until she was forced to resign.

Key Incidents

Hidden Redundancies and Uninformed Staff: Karla discovered that former staff had been made redundant and quietly relocated to back offices. Her current team had never been told she was their supervisor.

Why it occurred: Lack of transparency and leadership avoidance.

Appearance-Based Hiring and Self-Consciousness: Karla noticed the clinic's hiring practices favoured slim, blonde, conventionally attractive women. She began to feel hyper-aware of her appearance and fearful of non-acceptance.

Why it occurred: A discriminatory culture prioritising image over competence.

Theatre Sabotage and Physical Intimidation: Karla was sent to manage theatre operations without training. During one shift, Tom threw heavy magazines at her head. He was later terminated.

Why it occurred: Hostility from displaced staff and lack of supervision.

Documentation Theft and Operational Sabotage: Karla prepared contracts, wristbands, and labels for 65 surgical patients; the materials were stolen. Leadership provided no assistance or accountability.

Why it occurred: Malicious interference and managerial indifference.

Dual Roles and Unpaid Labour: Karla was required to manage both theatre and reception without additional pay. Colleagues refused to collaborate with difficult staff, leaving her to shoulder the workload.

Why it occurred: Exploitation through inequitable workload distribution.

Switchboard Sabotage and Final Confrontation: Anne repeatedly called and hung up on the switchboard to make it appear Karla was missing calls. Karla confronted her on her final day.

Why it occurred: Targeted reputational sabotage.

Impact on the Victim

Karla experienced:

- Physical illness, including gastroenteritis and shingles
- Psychological distress, anxiety, and chronic workplace fear
- Erosion of trust in leadership and loss of professional confidence
- Interrupted career trajectory and financial instability

Therapeutic and Legal Analysis

Karla's experience meets Safe Work Australia's definition of workplace bullying — repeated, unreasonable behaviour creating a risk to health and safety.

Key breaches included:

- Physical intimidation and psychological harassment
- Systemic failure to intervene despite visible dysfunction
- Unsafe workload expectations and managerial negligence
- The clinic's leadership failed to create a psychologically safe environment. Their inaction enabled known bullies and perpetuated a culture of fear and silence.

Protective Framing for Publication

This case study reflects Karla's lived experience. To protect against defamation:

- No formal misconduct charges were laid.
- Events are described from the victim's perspective.
- Names, roles, and details have been anonymised or altered.

Professional Commentary

Karla's case highlights the human cost of aesthetic-based hiring, absent leadership, and unchecked sabotage. Her resilience in managing dual portfolios amid open hostility exemplifies professional integrity under duress.

Her story is a call for reform within private healthcare administration — where competence must outweigh image, and psychological safety must be embedded in policy, not just promised in mission statements.

Interlude: From Private Harm to Public Systems

What begins as a private injury rarely stays private.

The wound moves — from the body to the workplace, from one organisation to the next, until it becomes embedded in systems that mistake silence for order.

The stories that came before — of individuals bullied, scapegoated, or erased — reveal something deeper than personal cruelty. They expose structural blindness.

They show how institutions designed to protect people can, when left unchecked, perpetuate harm in quieter, more bureaucratic forms.

When workplaces fail to intervene, they do not remain neutral. They become complicit.

A single act of sabotage becomes policy when management ignores it.

A single voice dismissed becomes a culture when silence is rewarded.

This is how harm scales.

It travels through hiring practices that prioritise convenience over conscience.

It hides behind performance reviews, HR jargon, and mission statements that praise "resilience" while punishing truth.

It thrives where trauma is mislabelled as "personality conflict," and bullying is rebranded as "management style."

But harm, when named, becomes data.

And data, when witnessed, becomes reform.

These next stories shift the lens from individual experience to systemic accountability.

They are not only about the people who were hurt, but about the cultures that allowed it — the structures that reward manipulation, the hierarchies that silence dissent, and the institutions that mistake compliance for harmony.

This is where private harm becomes public evidence.

Where the pattern becomes undeniable.

Where reform is no longer optional, but inevitable.

Case Study: Michelle

TOXIC LEADERSHIP AND PSYCHOLOGICAL INJURY

When abuse becomes policy and neglect is framed as "process," harm evolves — no longer personal, but procedural.

Michelle's experience within a government department exemplifies this evolution. It was not a single act of cruelty that broke her, but a system that normalised it.

Background

Michelle entered a front-line administrative role that had already cycled through multiple staff due to dysfunction and bullying. The environment was marked by toxic leadership, remote supervision, and a culture of fear disguised as professionalism.

She accepted the position hoping for stability — a quieter chapter after years in high-pressure environments. Instead, she found herself navigating a system that rewarded compliance over competence, silence over integrity, and endurance over wellbeing.

Incident Overview

Over time, Michelle endured sustained psychological abuse from her supervisor and director, followed by reputational sabotage and exclusion under a new team leader.

The mistreatment began as subtle condescension and control, later escalating into open hostility, gaslighting, and systemic neglect. Despite her diligence, competence, and professionalism, Michelle was repeatedly undermined. Her every attempt to seek clarity or fairness was reframed as defiance.

The cumulative effect was emotional exhaustion, professional stagnation, and profound loss of trust.

Key Incidents

Remote Supervision and Initial Abuse: Michelle received no training and was left to manage complex administrative processes alone. Her remote supervisor, Bella, criticised her without context and later misrepresented her performance to the director.
Why it occurred: Lack of onboarding, blurred accountability, and a power alliance that prioritised loyalty over competence.

Threats and Psychological Manipulation: The director summoned Michelle to a private meeting and threatened to terminate her employment unless she "got along with Bella." Her concerns about mistreatment were dismissed outright.
Why it occurred: Abuse of authority and protection of a toxic hierarchy.

Team Dysfunction and DEI Exploitation: Several staff neglected their duties, exploited diversity and equity hiring protections, and formed exclusionary cliques. Michelle was left to carry the workload without recognition or relief.
Why it occurred: Poor leadership and systemic misuse of inclusion policies to shield underperformance.

Leadership Change and Continued Targeting: After the director and Bella left, Pamela was appointed as team leader. Having been briefed negatively about Michelle, Pamela immediately began excluding her from meetings and discussions.

Why it occurred: Prejudiced handover and personal insecurity.

Interview Panel Exclusion and Role Undermining: Michelle was removed from an interview panel without consultation, violating the team's collaborative governance structure.
Why it occurred: Assertion of dominance and targeted exclusion.

Surveillance and Personal Intrusion: Pamela followed Michelle around the office, attempted to overhear a personal phone call, and repeatedly invaded her physical space.
Why it occurred: Control tactics driven by envy and insecurity.

Contract Expiry and Exit Sabotage: Upon deciding not to renew her contract, Michelle was accused of abandoning her post without notice — a false claim that further damaged her reputation.
Why it occurred: Retaliation and vindictive reputation management.

Impact on the Victim
Michelle experienced significant emotional and physical consequences, including:

- Chronic anxiety, sleep disruption, and fatigue
- Workplace isolation and deterioration of self-worth
- Reputational harm within her department
- Loss of trust in leadership and institutional systems
- Relief upon resignation — tempered by lingering psychological injury

Her withdrawal was not resignation from work, but from harm.

Therapeutic and Legal Analysis
Michelle's experience meets Safe Work Australia's definition of workplace bullying and psychological injury. It reflects:

- Repeated, unreasonable behaviour creating a health and safety risk
- Threats, exclusion, and reputational sabotage
- Breaches of procedural fairness and psychological safety
- The organisation's failure to implement trauma-informed supervision and transparent oversight enabled the abuse to persist unchecked. Michelle's departure, though painful, represented an act of self-preservation.

Protective Framing for Publication

This case study represents Michelle's lived experience. To ensure ethical and legal integrity:

- No formal misconduct findings were recorded against individuals named.
- Events are presented from the victim's documented perspective.
- Names, departments, and identifying details have been altered or anonymised.
- Interpretations are therapeutic and educational in nature.

Professional Commentary

Michelle's case illustrates the quiet devastation wrought by toxic leadership normalised as administrative routine. It exposes how bureaucratic systems — when unaccountable — can perpetuate psychological harm under the guise of policy.
Her story underscores the urgent need for:

- Trauma-informed management training
- Transparent and fair DEI implementation
- Mechanisms for reporting retaliation and psychological abuse

Michelle's decision to step away was not weakness — it was clarity.

Her courage in naming the dysfunction invites reform not just within one office, but across the culture of public service itself.

INTERLUDE: **From Evidence to Accountability**

Naming harm is only the beginning.

The real work begins when evidence demands response — when systems can no longer hide behind paperwork, hierarchy, or polite indifference.

What this case studies reveal is not a handful of isolated incidents, but a pattern of institutional neglect.

Policies existed. Procedures existed. But the will to act — to intervene, to protect, to believe — did not.

Accountability begins where denial ends.

It begins when leadership stops mistaking avoidance for neutrality.

When HR stops treating trauma as inconvenience.

When policy becomes more than a shield for liability — when it becomes a tool for justice.

These stories are more than mere cautionary tales.

They are data points in a wider failure — evidence of cultures that normalise dysfunction and punish truth-telling.

Each complaint dismissed, each report ignored, each whisper down a corridor is part of a larger map of harm.

To study these stories is to confront a truth many institutions resist:

that abuse thrives not because of bad people alone, but because of good systems unwilling to see themselves clearly.

Accountability is not about blame — it is about integrity.

It asks, *what does it mean to lead ethically when the truth is uncomfortable?*

It asks, *what are we protecting — our people, or our image?*

The reckoning ahead is not only professional. It is moral.

For the measure of any system — whether hospital, agency, or boardroom — is not its mission statement, but how it treats the most vulnerable within its walls.

The following case marks this turning point.

It moves beyond the single story into the shared pattern — beyond silence, into system.

From evidence, we move now to accountability.

In the wake of these patterns, one story stands out for the depth of its betrayal — a reminder that even when we leave a toxic workplace, the architecture of harm can follow us across systems, through networks, and into new beginnings.

Case Study: Hattie

THE BETRAYAL WITHIN AND PSYCHOLOGICAL INJURY

Background

Hattie accepted a role at a community organisation that closely mirrored her previous not-for-profit mental health position. The salary was higher, and on paper, it appeared to offer stability and alignment with her values. Yet, she hesitated — her previous workplace had been toxic, and the trauma was still fresh.

Unbeknownst to her, the new organisation had direct connections to her former employer through overlapping staff and management networks. This unacknowledged link breached confidentiality and set the stage for renewed psychological harm.

Incident Overview

From her first weeks, Hattie encountered coordinated bullying, reputational sabotage, and emotional abuse. Colleagues aligned with her previous workplace began spreading misinformation, excluding her from key communications, and undermining her authority.

Despite her professionalism and consistent work ethic, Hattie became the target of a sustained campaign of hostility and discrediting that ultimately forced her resignation.

Key Incidents

Hostile Welcome and Refusal to Train: Administrative staff members Sandra and Jaqueen refused to train Hattie, opting to work from home for extended periods while expressing resentment over her appointment.
Why it occurred: Loyalty to the previous staff member and resistance to change.

False Instructions and Gaslighting: Jaqueen deliberately gave Hattie incorrect instructions, later denied doing so, and accused her of fabricating details.
Why it occurred: Manipulation, control, and a calculated attempt to destabilise Hattie's confidence.

Professional Initiative and Jealousy: Hattie initiated a collaboration meeting with a local Women's Health Centre. Her initiative was met with hostility and jealousy from Jaqueen.
Why it occurred: Professional envy and territorial insecurity.

Misinformation and Alliance Sabotage: Jaqueen spread false narratives about Hattie, influencing colleagues and the payroll officer, Jennifer. A small faction formed to isolate and undermine her.
Why it occurred: Coordinated bullying and reputational sabotage reinforced by management silence.

Racial Targeting and Narcissistic Abuse: Tonka made racially charged comments toward Hattie and engaged in narcissistic manipulation. A colleague nicknamed "Spylogical Boy" enabled this behaviour.
Why it occurred: Racial bias, narcissistic behaviour, and leadership failure to intervene.

Performance Management and Public Intimidation:
Klodine lodged a complaint, triggering a disciplinary meeting.
Hattie was summoned without notice, denied support, and had her
emails projected publicly in a display designed to shame and intimidate her.
Why it occurred: Escalated bullying and procedural misconduct
aimed at silencing her.

Impact on the Victim
Hattie experienced profound and cumulative harm:

- Physical symptoms including migraines, insomnia, and
  exhaustion
- Severe emotional distress and workplace anxiety
- Breach of confidentiality and reputational damage
- Long-term loss of professional trust and stability

Therapeutic and Legal Analysis
Hattie's experience meets Safe Work Australia's definition of workplace bullying and psychological injury.

Key breaches included:

- Repeated, unreasonable behaviour creating risk to health
  and safety
- Racial discrimination and reputational sabotage
- Breach of confidentiality and procedural fairness

From a therapeutic perspective:

- The bullying displayed patterns of narcissistic group
  behaviour and racial targeting.
- Hattie's trauma symptoms — insomnia, hypervigilance,
  and withdrawal — are consistent with prolonged
  exposure to psychological abuse.

- The organisation's failure to investigate or act decisively constituted a systemic breach of duty of care.

Protective Framing for Publication
This case study reflects Hattie's lived experience. To protect against defamation:

- No formal misconduct findings were issued.
- Events are described from the victim's documented and corroborated perspective.
- Names and organisational identifiers have been anonymised or fictionalised.

Professional Commentary
Hattie's case exposes the hidden dangers of inter-organisational alliances and unregulated confidentiality breaches within the community and mental health sectors.

When former employers and new workplaces are socially or professionally linked, survivors of workplace trauma are left vulnerable to re-exposure and retraumatisation.

Her experience underscores the need for:

- Clear boundaries around cross-agency communication
- Cultural safety frameworks that address racial bias
- Trauma-informed leadership to prevent the weaponisation of networks and narratives

Hattie's experience reveals how harm does not end with resignation — it migrates, mutates, and reappears through networks of silence and shared denial.

Her story marks the threshold between private suffering and public accountability, where systems must be examined, not just individuals. What follows turns outward — from the personal to the institutional, from the testimony of harm to the blueprint for reform.

WEAPONISED LOYALTY

"In toxic workplaces, loyalty
isn't earned — it's rewarded
for betrayal."

— Veronica Ruff

Interlude: From Accountability to Reform

Accountability is not the end of the story. It is where the story begins to turn.

Each case study has illuminated what happens when silence becomes policy — when leadership mistakes loyalty for ethics, and when systems protect their image instead of their people. But accountability without reform is performance. It is damage control dressed as progress.

What follows is not about blame. It is about architecture — the redesign of workplaces, policies, and leadership cultures that have normalised harm. It asks harder questions:

- What would change if trauma-informed leadership were the standard, not the exception?
- What if whistleblowing were not a risk, but a protected right?
- What if workplaces were built on clarity, dignity, and truth — rather than compliance and fear?

Reform is not an abstract idea. It begins in every meeting where someone names what others deny, every policy rewritten with compassion, every conversation that restores humanity to systems that lost it.

The chapters that follow move beyond testimony. They move into transformation — from evidence to ethics, from reckoning to redesign.

This isn't merely a call for accountability.

It is a blueprint for change.

Case Study: Annette

Background

Annette accepted a temporary receptionist position at an equipment hire company that had recently merged five regional branches into one large site. The new role combined administration, logistics, and facilities management, including responsibility for the cleaning contract, stock ordering, and coordinating truck drivers.

Although the position promised stability and professional growth, Annette soon discovered a culture steeped in manipulation, favouritism, and covert hostility. What appeared to be an operational challenge was, in reality, a workplace defined by control, secrecy, and emotional harm.

Incident Overview

Over several months, Annette endured repeated sabotage, public humiliation, and reputational harm. Her attempts to improve workplace processes were met with hostility from management and peers. The culture was dominated by cliques, unethical leadership, and surveillance disguised as oversight.

Despite her diligence and professionalism, Annette was systematically undermined, scapegoated for systemic failures, and ultimately forced to leave the role to protect her wellbeing.

Key Incidents

Cleaning Contract Contradictions: Tasked with resolving ongoing cleaning issues, Annette raised legitimate concerns supported by staff complaints. While initially encouraged by management, she was later publicly contradicted and accused of fabricating problems.
Why it occurred: Avoidance of accountability and manipulative leadership seeking to preserve image over integrity.

Coffee Theft and Financial Mismanagement: Annette discovered excessive coffee orders and suspected internal theft. Her attempts to introduce cost controls were dismissed, and she was mocked for suggesting accountability measures.
Why it occurred: Entitlement, poor oversight, and resistance to transparency.

Training Sabotage and Denied Access: Annette was deliberately excluded from training on company systems. Designated trainers withheld access, forcing her to seek guidance externally.
Why it occurred: Favouritism and deliberate obstruction to reinforce hierarchy.

Public Humiliation and Scapegoating: Following a client complaint caused by communication failures, Annette was yelled at in front of staff and customers. Leadership ignored context and blamed her publicly.
Why it occurred: Deflection of responsibility and culture of intimidation.

Repeated Stock Orders and Suspected Theft: Annette was instructed to reorder stock she had already purchased. The pattern suggested misappropriation, but her concerns were dismissed.

Why it occurred: Negligence and possible theft enabled by managerial indifference.

Exposure of Favouritism: During an exit interview, a staff member revealed an inappropriate relationship between the manager and Virginia. Virginia was quietly reassigned.
Why it occurred: Ethical breaches and conflict of interest masked by managerial collusion.

Final Escalation and Forced Departure: After expressing frustration about poor communication, Annette was yelled at in front of several office staff. She contacted her agency and requested immediate release from her contract.
Why it occurred: Retaliation and reputation management.

Impact on the Victim
Annette experienced:

- Psychological distress and emotional exhaustion
- Loss of professional confidence and trust in management
- Repeated public humiliation and scapegoating
- Reputational harm and withdrawal from corporate environments

Therapeutic and Legal Analysis
Annette's experience meets Safe Work Australia's definition of workplace bullying and psychological injury. The organisation failed to uphold its duty of care by allowing repeated, unreasonable behaviour that placed her mental health and safety at risk.
Key breaches included:

- Persistent public humiliation and reputational damage
- Denial of training and access to essential systems
- Abuse of authority and procedural misconduct

The company's tolerance of unethical leadership and unchecked favouritism reflects systemic dysfunction and a disregard for psychological safety.

Protective Framing for Publication

This case study reflects Annette's lived experience. To protect against defamation:

- No formal misconduct findings were recorded.
- All events are described from the victim's perspective.
- Names, titles, and identifying details have been anonymised.

Professional Commentary

Annette's story highlights the dangers of unchecked managerial power, workplace favouritism, and retaliatory behaviour in corporate environments.

Her experience underscores the urgent need for:

- Trauma-informed leadership training
- Transparent accountability structures
- Zero-tolerance policies for bullying and scapegoating

Annette's professionalism in the face of systemic abuse is both courageous and instructive. Her story stands as a warning to organisations that value optics over ethics — and a reminder that psychological safety is not optional.

GASLIGHTING
RED FLAGS

"Gaslighting doesn't start
with shouting — it starts
with doubt. With the
slow erosion of your
certainty, until you apologise
for things you never did."

— Veronica Ruff

Case Study: Simone

ALLIED HEALTH CLINIC AND PSYCHOLOGICAL INJURY

Background

Simone began a new role at an allied health clinic, working weekday shifts from 11 a.m. to 7 p.m. She was promised thorough training and collegial support from two administrative staff members. Instead, she was met with exclusion, sabotage, and sustained psychological abuse.

Incident Overview

From the outset, Simone was deliberately obstructed, isolated, and undermined. Her training was withheld, her competence was questioned, and her wellbeing steadily eroded. Over time, the cumulative impact of the bullying led to psychological injury and professional withdrawal.

Key Incidents

Withheld Training and Isolation:

Simone was promised hands-on training but was deliberately excluded and left alone for extended periods.

Why it occurred: Territorial behaviour, insecurity, and resistance to new staff.

Contradictory Instructions and Gaslighting: Yvetta provided inconsistent, incorrect instructions, then reprimanded Simone for following them.
Why it occurred: Manipulative control tactics and fear of professional comparison.

Exclusion and Degrading Tasks: Simone was ostracised from team discussions and given menial tasks that others were not required to perform.
Why it occurred: Power imbalance, jealousy, and targeted humiliation.

Public Berating Over Pest-Control Task:
Simone was publicly reprimanded for failing to complete a task despite not being provided the necessary information.
Why it occurred: Intentional setup and performative shaming.

Final Confrontation and Departure:
Simone confronted Yvetta about her behaviour and resigned immediately.
Why it occurred: Cumulative psychological harm and professional sabotage.

Impact on the Victim
Simone experienced:

- Sleep disturbance, anxiety, and emotional exhaustion.
- Erosion of confidence and professional identity.
- Workplace isolation and reputational harm.
- Long-term psychological injury consistent with trauma exposure.

Therapeutic and Legal Analysis
Simone's experience meets Safe Work Australia's definition of workplace bullying — repeated, unreasonable behaviour creating a risk to health and safety.

Key breaches included:

- Withholding of essential training and support.
- Delegation of degrading or exclusionary tasks.
- Public humiliation and reputational sabotage.
- The organisation failed to ensure a psychologically safe workplace, enabling known bullies to operate unchecked.

Protective Framing for Publication

This case study reflects Simone's lived experience. To protect against defamation:

- No formal misconduct charges were laid.
- Events are described from the victim's perspective.
- Names and roles have been anonymised or fictionalised where appropriate.

Professional Commentary

Simone's case exposes how territorial bullying and manipulative "training" practices can devastate morale and identity within care-based professions. Her decision to leave was not weakness — it was a decisive act of self-preservation and truth-telling.

Her experience underscores the urgent need for ethical onboarding, trauma-informed supervision, and psychologically safe clinical environments where dignity and integrity are non-negotiable.

The final case studies close the circle of testimony — voices once silenced now speaking into a collective record of truth. What follows is not just reflection, but reconstruction: the beginning of transformation.

Interlude

FROM TESTIMONY TO TRANSFORMATION

Every story you've just read began as a whisper — a quiet record of harm, disbelief, and survival.

Each case carried the same refrain: *This is not how work should feel.*

The testimonies are not isolated tragedies. They are data.

They reveal patterns that cross industries, sectors, and hierarchies — patterns of manipulation rewarded, truth punished, and silence institutionalised.

Each survivor became both witness and evidence.

Their pain charted the same fault lines:

– Workplaces that valued optics over integrity.

– Leaders who mistook dominance for direction.

– Systems that confused compliance with care.

These are not individual failures.

They are the inevitable outcomes of cultures built on fear, competition, and control.

But testimony alone is not enough.

Stories name the wound; transformation tends the healing.

To change what we have seen, we must move from recognition to reconstruction — from the personal to the systemic, from empathy to architecture.

Transformation begins when we treat truth as infrastructure.

When policy becomes protection, not performance.

When leadership is measured not by authority, but by accountability.

When workplaces evolve from psychological minefields into sanctuaries of safety and respect.

The pages that follow turn outward.

They move from lived experience to structural reform — from what broke, to what must be built.

They ask: *What does repair look like in practice?*

What would a trauma-informed workplace truly feel like?

How can policy, ethics, and empathy coexist — not as ideals, but as standards?

This is where the reckoning becomes redesign.

Where testimony becomes blueprint.

Where silence gives way to structure — and truth, finally, has a home.

The Architecture of Change

Reform does not begin in policy rooms.

It begins in the spaces where harm was once normalised — in the silences that survivors refused to keep, in the documents rewritten with truth instead of optics, in the ordinary workplaces where someone finally said, *"Enough."*

The architecture of change is built from reckoning, not rhetoric.

It is not a glossy report or a motivational slogan. It is the daily, disciplined work of dismantling systems that protect power and rebuilding ones that protect people.

Every reform begins with a truth-teller.

Every culture shift begins with a listener who refuses to look away.

And every new structure begins with the humility to ask: *Who has been harmed by the way we work — and how do we make sure it never happens again?*

1. **From Compliance to Care**

Most organisations pride themselves on compliance.

Few practises care.

Compliance asks, "What must we do to avoid liability?"

Care asks, "What must we do to ensure safety?"

Compliance is performative; care is transformative.

True reform demands that we move beyond checklists and toward compassion. That we see psychological safety not as a legal requirement but as a moral and cultural imperative.

This shift requires leaders who are fluent in empathy — who understand that safeguarding wellbeing is not a soft skill, but a strategic necessity.

Care-driven systems are built on three foundations:

- **Transparency:** Clarity in communication and accountability.
- **Consistency:** Fair application of policies across all levels.
- **Courage:** Willingness to act when harm is identified, even when inconvenient.

Without these, compliance becomes a theatre of protection for the institution, not the individual.

2. Trauma-Informed Leadership

The future of leadership is trauma-informed.

This means leading with awareness that people carry unseen injuries — from workplaces, from histories, from systems that punished truth.

It means rejecting the myth of "professional distance" when that distance enables cruelty.

Trauma-informed leaders:

- Recognise signs of distress before they escalate.
- Respond with curiosity, not defensiveness.
- Repair with accountability, not avoidance.

Such leadership does not ask, "What's wrong with you?" but,

"What happened to you — and how can we ensure it never happens again here?"

Organisations must embed this approach into supervision, conflict resolution, and performance management. Otherwise, they risk perpetuating cycles of harm while branding themselves as "progressive."

3. **Redesigning Accountability**

Accountability must evolve from punishment to prevention.

In traditional systems, accountability is reactive — it surfaces only after harm has occurred, often to manage optics.

In trauma-informed systems, accountability is proactive — it lives in the culture, the communication, the everyday courage to name and address dysfunction early.

To redesign accountability:

- **Audit the silences.** Examine the complaints that were minimised or retracted under pressure.
- **Redefine leadership metrics.** Reward ethical conduct and psychological safety, not just output.
- **Create independent pathways for reporting.** Ensure that those investigating harm are not entangled in its perpetuation.

True accountability is not an HR exercise — it is a cultural ethos. It exists when people no longer whisper truth in corridors but can speak it in meetings without fear.

4. **Ethical Architecture**

Systems that protect truth must be intentionally designed.

Ethical architecture is the blueprint for this — it integrates integrity into structure, not just sentiment.

This involves:

- **Trauma-informed induction and training** for all staff, including managers.
- **Independent wellbeing oversight** with authority to intervene.
- **Restorative processes** that prioritise healing over retaliation.
- **Leadership succession planning** that values character as much as competence.

Ethical architecture asks: *Who benefits from the current design — and who is harmed by it?*

Only when those questions are answered honestly can reform move from aspiration to action.

5. **The Cultural Equation**

Culture is not what's written on the wall — it's what happens when no one is watching.

Toxic cultures thrive in ambiguity, in blurred boundaries and whispered complicity.

Reformed cultures thrive in clarity — where communication is transparent, behaviour is consistent, and silence is no longer a survival strategy.

Cultural transformation requires:

- **Ongoing reflection:** Regular reviews of team dynamics and leadership impact.
- **Psychological literacy:** Training to understand trauma, projection, and emotional regulation.
- **Inclusive design:** Systems built with diverse voices, not merely represented but empowered.

Culture shifts when people no longer trade empathy for advancement — when safety becomes the standard, not the exception.

. . .

6. **From Policy to Praxis**

Every policy must have a pulse.

Policies written without lived experience risk becoming monuments to good intention.

Praxis — the alignment of values with action — requires continual consultation with those most affected by systemic failure.

To move from policy to praxis:

- Involve survivors in reform design.
- Ground decisions in evidence from lived experience, not assumption.
- Measure success not by absence of complaints, but by presence of trust.

Policy without practice protects reputation.
Praxis protects people.

7. **The Legacy of Structural Courage**

The architecture of change is not built overnight. It is built through courage layered over time.

Each act of truth-telling becomes a foundation.

Each intervention becomes a beam.

Each policy written in compassion becomes a wall that holds others safely.

And one day, when the old systems collapse under the weight of their denial, these new structures will stand — quiet, steady, and strong.

They will not need to perform integrity.

They will embody it.

Closing Reflection: Building Forward

Change begins when someone decides to design differently.

You have seen the cost of silence. You have seen the wreckage of unchecked power.

Now, you are part of the rebuilding.
You do not need to wait for permission to design systems that
honour truth.
You are the architect.

And this — this moment of clarity, courage, and compassion — is
where the foundation is laid.

PART V
Appendices

Blueprints for Reform

TURNING INSIGHT INTO INFRASTRUCTURE

Reform is not a slogan.

It is architecture — the invisible scaffolding that determines whether truth collapses or holds.

What begins as testimony must evolve into structure. Without structure, even the clearest reckoning dissolves back into rhetoric.

This chapter translates the principles of accountability, trauma-informed practice, and psychological safety into tangible frameworks for workplaces, institutions, and systems.117

It is an invitation to rebuild — not from scratch, but from integrity.

1. The Foundation: Psychological Safety as Policy

Psychological safety must move from aspiration to regulation.

It cannot depend on the empathy of a single leader or the mood of a team; it must be embedded in governance.

A trauma-informed organisation:

- Embeds *wellbeing risk assessments* alongside physical-safety audits.
- Includes *psychological injury* within every incident-reporting process.
- Protects truth-tellers through *whistle-blower frameworks* that are actually enforceable.
- Requires *leaders* to be trained in recognising manipulation, gaslighting, and covert abuse.
- Holds *managers* accountable for the emotional climate they create, not just the metrics they meet.

Accountability is not punitive — it is protective.
The aim isn't to achieve perfection, but to cultivate awareness.

2. The Design: Ethical Leadership

Leadership is the most powerful determinant of workplace health.

Ethical leadership is not about charisma; it is about consistency.

Blueprints for ethical leadership include:

- Transparent communication: clarity before comfort.
- Boundaried compassion: care that does not collude with harm.
- Reflective supervision: spaces where leaders are required to examine their own behaviour.
- Restorative practice: addressing harm through acknowledgement, reparation, and prevention — not silence.

True leaders are not those who avoid discomfort, but those who can sit inside it without retaliation.

3. The Framework: Trauma-Informed Governance

Institutions must learn to read harm systemically rather than individually.

Key components:

1. **Education** – All staff receive training in trauma dynamics, unconscious bias, and power misuse.
2. **Accountability Pathways** – Multiple reporting routes (internal, external, anonymous) ensure safety.
3. **Independent Oversight** – Investigations led by neutral experts, not by peers with conflicts of interest.
4. **Restorative Review Boards** – Panels that examine not only what happened but *why the system allowed it.*

Governance that cannot hold complexity will always protect the powerful.

4. The Blueprint in Practice: From Policy to Culture

Culture change requires repetition, ritual, and reward.

Every meeting, memo, and metric must signal that wellbeing is not optional.

Examples of reform in action:

- **Healthcare:** Debriefing models integrated into every shift; managers trained in vicarious-trauma response.
- **Public Service:** Independent psychological-safety ombudsman; mandatory ethics reviews for promotions.
- **Education:** Anti-bullying policies expanded to include staff-to-staff psychological abuse.
- **Not-for-Profit:** Culture of care must replace the culture of image. Transparent governance, ethical leadership audits, and accountability for public funds restore purpose where hypocrisy once thrived. Reform

begins when compassion is no longer used as camouflage for exploitation.

- **Corporate:** Performance appraisals include metrics for empathy, communication, and accountability.

Policies are only as powerful as the cultures that animate them.

Change becomes sustainable when safety is rewarded as visibly as productivity.

Across every sector — profit or purpose, private or public — the same truth remains:

Systems are only as ethical as the people who lead them, and leadership is only as humane as the culture that sustains it. Reform does not begin with slogans or strategy, but with the daily decision to choose integrity over image.

Real change does not arrive through policy manuals or polished statements — it arrives when people inside the system begin to act differently. When empathy becomes procedural, when account-ability replaces avoidance, when the quiet voices are finally heard — that is when reform stops being theory and becomes culture.

5. The Human Element: Restorative Systems

Every reform must include restoration — not just compliance.

Restorative systems recognise that:

- Harm requires acknowledgement before correction.
- Survivors need participation in repair, not exclusion from it.
- Collective healing is strategic, not sentimental.

When organisations model apology, transparency, and learning, they transform from defensive bureaucracies into ethical communities.

Restoration begins where blame ends. It asks: *What would repair look like if we centred humanity instead of liability?* It requires conversations that are uncomfortable but honest — apologies that name the harm, not just the policy breach. Restorative systems create space for survivors to shape the reform process itself, transforming pain into prevention.

When workplaces learn to hold truth without retaliation, the culture shifts. Not because of new policies or slogans, but because people feel safe enough to tell the truth. And once that happens, real accountability — and real healing — can begin.

When restoration becomes part of the culture, dignity returns to the centre of work — and from that centre, everything healthy grows.

6. Measuring What Matters

We measure what we value.

If all metrics reward efficiency, cruelty will always be cost-effective.

Reform means adding new measures of success:

- Staff retention after trauma disclosure.
- Psychological-safety scores from anonymous surveys.
- Diversity not only in hiring but in *decision-making power.*
- Reduction in formal grievances due to early intervention.

Numbers do not tell the whole story — but they can signal whether an organisation is evolving or repeating its past.

7. Closing Reflection: The Blueprint and the Breath

Reform begins with structure but survives through breath — the daily, human act of alignment.

Every conversation, policy, and performance review is a chance to choose clarity over collusion.

Every survivor who speaks rewires the system for those who follow.

Blueprints are not blueprints for buildings; they are blueprints for belonging.

They remind us that safety is not a privilege — it is a principle.

This chapter ends where true leadership begins:
with the courage to build what should have existed all along.

The Future of Work and Healing

From Survival to Evolution

Reform builds the scaffolding.

Healing animates it.

The future of work will not be defined by new job titles or hybrid schedules, but by whether organisations can become places where nervous systems can exhale — where productivity and humanity coexist without collision.

We are entering an era where trauma literacy is leadership currency, where empathy is infrastructure, and where silence is finally recognised as an occupational hazard.

1. From Repair to Renewal

Reform stabilises what was broken. Renewal imagines what has never existed.

The next evolution of workplace culture must move beyond compliance toward consciousness.

Renewal asks:

- What if productivity meant *presence* rather than exhaustion?
- What if leadership meant *attunement* rather than control?
- What if policies measured *how* we work, not just *what* we produce?

This shift is not theoretical. It is physiological. When people feel safe, they think more clearly, collaborate more deeply, and create more freely. Safety is not sentimental — it is strategic.

2. Trauma-Informed Workplaces as the New Standard

The most progressive organisations of the coming decade will treat psychological safety as core infrastructure.

They will:

- **Normalise nervous-system awareness** in meetings and performance reviews.
- **Integrate trauma-responsive design** into architecture, workflow, and communication.
- **Redefine success** to include sustainability, rest, and relational integrity.
- **Invest in prevention** through supervision, reflection, and debriefing, not crisis management.

Workplaces that honour humanity will outperform those that exploit it.

Not because empathy is fashionable — but because it is efficient.

3. Leadership as Healing Practice

The future leader is part strategist, part steward.

Their role is not to fix, but to *facilitate repair*.

They practise:

- **Transparent humility** — admitting when they cause harm.
- **Regulated leadership** — responding, not reacting.
- **Relational accountability** — measuring success by collective wellbeing.

When leaders model self-reflection, they create permission for honesty.

When they embody calm, they recalibrate entire cultures.

4. Collective Healing as Organisational Strategy

Healing at work is not indulgence; it is intelligence.

Teams that process conflict restore energy faster than those that repress it.

The new workplace will prioritise:

- **Restorative conversations** instead of silent resignations.
- **Reflective supervision** instead of punitive performance plans.
- **Peer-support networks** instead of gossip and isolation.

Collective healing replaces shame with shared learning — the true metric of progress.

5. Technology, Humanity, and Boundaries

As automation expands, the challenge is not efficiency — it is empathy.

Artificial intelligence can optimise workflow, but only humans can create safety.

Boundaries will become the next revolution: knowing when to disconnect, when to breathe, when to protect the mind that powers the machine.

Digital wellbeing policies must evolve from token gestures to structural norms: scheduled no-meeting hours, right-to-disconnect clauses, and recognition of cognitive fatigue as legitimate strain.

6. The Economics of Dignity

Future economies will reward organisations that honour dignity as a measurable asset.

Burnout costs billions; belonging multiplies value.

Investors and regulators are beginning to see that ethical governance and employee safety are not opposites — they are identical goals expressed at different scales.

The sustainable organisation of tomorrow will not ask, *how much can we extract?*

It will ask, *how much can we sustain?*

7. The Evolution of Language

As systems evolve, so must the words we use.

- "Human resources" becomes **human relations.**

- "Performance management" becomes **growth dialogue.**
- "Exit interview" becomes **completion reflection.**

Language does not just describe culture — it creates it. When we speak differently, we lead differently.

8. Closing Reflection: The Work That Heals

The future of work is not built in boardrooms; it is born in every decision to choose clarity over compliance, compassion over convenience, accountability over avoidance.

Healing, like leadership, is iterative — a daily negotiation between courage and care.

Each survivor who re-enters a workplace carries the blueprint for something better.

Each leader who listens without defence plants a seed of cultural repair.

The systems we build next will not be perfect.

But they can be conscious.

And consciousness, sustained over time, becomes culture.

This is the threshold — where work becomes restoration, and restoration becomes the new standard.

Epilogue: The Reckoning That Writes Itself

The stories you have read are not isolated events.

They are patterns — woven through workplaces, institutions, and generations.

They are echoes of the same choreography: power without accountability, silence mistaken for professionalism, cruelty disguised as care.

But something else runs beneath every story here — something the system could not erase.

Clarity.

Integrity.

Voice.

Each testimony in these pages is more than evidence. It is reclamation.

It is the moment where silence ends and legacy begins —

where survival turns into authorship.

Healing from betrayal is not about returning to who you were before.

It is about remembering who you are *beyond* what was done to you.

Every chapter has traced that evolution — from silence to speech, from fragmentation to sovereignty, from harm to meaning.

There is no single moment when justice arrives.

But there are moments of awakening — small, luminous recognitions that mark your way home.

The first time you name what happened without apology.

The first time you say no and feel no guilt.

The first time you realise that peace is not found in their approval, but in your own alignment.

That is the quiet revolution this book has documented:

not the fall of systems, but the rise of self-trust.

And as that trust deepens — individually, collectively — it reshapes the world of work itself.

Each person who refuses to disappear becomes a catalyst.

Each act of naming becomes a blueprint for reform.

This is how systems begin to heal — not from the top down, but from the inside out.

To those who have endured what others deny:

you are not defined by the harm, but by the truth you chose to tell about it.

Your clarity is not a threat — it is a form of leadership.

Your refusal to disappear is a form of resistance.

You have done what the system could not — you have borne witness.

You have told the truth.

And that truth will outlive every distortion.

This is the reckoning that writes itself —

one story, one name, one act of courage at a time.

The end is not silence.

It is authorship.

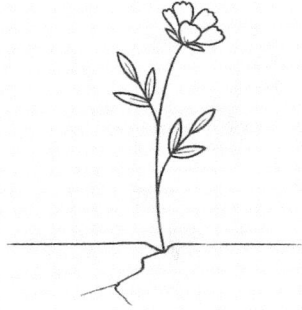

'Truth outlives
distortion.'

– Veronica Ruff

Author's Note: For Whoever Finds This

If you are holding these pages, you have already survived the hardest part — the disbelief.

The moment you first realised the harm was real. That it wasn't your fault. That your instincts were never the enemy.

You may still feel the tremors. You may still doubt your strength. But you are already doing the most courageous thing a survivor can do: telling yourself the truth.

This work draws from **composite lived experiences** — drawn together through years of reflection, documentation, and recovery. Every case, every insight, is rooted in real encounters with systems that failed to protect, and the long, quiet work of rebuilding what was taken.

While the names, settings, and details are anonymised for privacy and safety, the emotional truth remains untouched.

Healing is not loud. It happens in quiet choices — the boundaries you hold, the words you write, the rest you take without apology. It happens each time you choose dignity over distortion, clarity over confusion, self-trust over silence.

You're not falling behind; you're growing into who you're meant to be.

Your story is not over. It is unfolding — as testimony, as art, as legacy.

May these pages remind you that your voice matters.

That your clarity is sacred.

That what was taken does not define you — what you rebuild does.

You are not too much.

You are just finally free enough to be whole.

Colophon

When Work Becomes War: Healing from Workplace Bullying and Betrayal
Written, compiled, and designed by **Veronica Ruff**
All illustrations © **Veronica Ruff — Art & Text**

This work was created in dedication to survivors of workplace bullying and psychological injury.

Typeset in a contemporary serif font for readability and clarity.
Layout and design by **Veronica Ruff**
First Edition © 2025

www.ingramcontent.com/pod-product-compliance
Lightning Source LLC
Chambersburg PA
CBHW060039030426
42334CB00019B/2406